Crisis Points

Editors: Ian Taylor and Jock Young

The impact of the last decade of economic and political crisis in Britain appears to have dulled the nerve and commitment of the 'informed' political and social critic. 'Inevitable progress', 'benign capitalism', 'the politics of consensus' – the clichés of the 1960s are still paraded as the conventional wisdom of the 1980s. One consequence of this has been a dearth of informed and incisive discussion of issues such as the decline of educational, health and welfare services, the impact of inflation on living standards, physical fitness and nutrition and the everyday experience of poverty, illness, racism and crime in present-day Britain. This series focuses on the erosion of both the social and the political rights of the individual: for the decline in living standards is mirrored by the threat of new legislation and police powers to the freedom of the individual. Such a tightening of the reins of control has its cultural manifestation whether it is in the appearance of a new McCarthyism in the media and the universities or in the signs of resistance in youth culture and the new wave of popular music.

The Crisis Points series aims to rectify this gap in contemporary debate. The books are written from the inside by practitioners or activists confronting the crisis in their field of work; they are informed in their content, not academic in their style; and they are accessible to the increasing numbers of the public concerned with the social problems of our times. Above all they are short and provocative – a basis of debate, whether it be in the home, classroom or workplace.

Titles in the Crisis Points series

Published

The Devil Makes Work: Leisure in Capitalist Britain
John Clark and Chas Critcher

Schooling the Smash Street Kids
Paul Corrigan

Beyond Progressive Education
Ken Jones

Trapped within Welfare:
Surviving Social Work (2nd Edition)
Mike Simpkin

Forthcoming

Communications and Control
Graham Murdock

Schooling the
Smash Street Kids

Paul Corrigan

MACMILLAN

First published 1979
Reprinted 1981, 1982, 1983, 1985

Published by
MACMILLAN EDUCATION LTD
Houndmills, Basingstoke, Hampshire RG21 2XS
and London
Companies and representatives
throughout the world

Printed in Hong Kong

British Library Cataloguing in Publication Data

Corrigan, Paul
  Schooling the Smash Street Kids.
  —(Crisis points).
  1. Adolescent boys—England
  2. Labor and laboring class—England
  I. Title
  301.44′42   HQ799.G7

  ISBN 0-333-22076-5
  ISBN 0-333-22077-3 Pbk

Contents

Introduction   Researching social problems   1

1. Why bother to do research?   4
Sociological research – as she has been written   5
Doing research   7
Choosing research methods within a school   11
Methods used to get information about the
    boys' experience   13
Conclusion   16

2. Why do kids play truant?   18
My initial perceptions of education   18
What the boys think about school   22
Truancy – is it a question of values at all?   28
Why are schools compulsory? What are
    'schools'?   29
State education as imposition   30
The nature of education destined for the
    working class   33

3. Why do kids muck about in class?   45
Teachers as 'big-heads'   51
Understanding classroom interaction   56
Punishment and sanctions. What the school
    does when the campaign to win the hearts and
    minds of the working class fails . . .   61
Control in the classroom   66

4. Why do boys choose dead-end jobs? 72
Why choose certain jobs? 73
How do the boys see the whole job structure? 74
How do the boys see their future choice of work? 75
The boys' job expectations in relation to the
  way they see the job structure 81
The boys' perception of 'opportunity structures' 83
School, work and society 92

5. What do they get out of pop music and football? 93
How has sociology made sense of kids'
  spare-time activities? 94
Talking to the kids about their spare-time
  activities 97
Structured leisure activities 98
Commercial organisations 105
Why, then, do boys get into trouble? 116

6. Why do kids get into trouble on the street? 119
How 'doing nothing' when added to a 'weird
  idea' equals 'getting into trouble' 121

7. What you gonna do about it? 142
Youth, class and the state 142
The politics of research findings 142
Progressive education and 'educational
  turmoil' 143
Youth, class and revolutionary change 149

References 155

Introduction
Researching social problems

Yet another sociology book about the education of teenagers; yet another trendy left-wing treatise on what's wrong with everything; in writing this book it becomes obvious that there appears to be a surfeit of books about this topic already. The major reaction to the subject would be an uninterested glance from the general public and a groan of horror from those learning the sociology of education at yet another book on the reading list. Doubtless full of jargon and out of touch, leaving the teacher saying 'It's all very well for you to talk! YOU want to try coping with 4D on a Friday afternoon!' All of these reactions are well-founded in people's experience of the usefulness of sociology in coming to terms with their problems over the past twenty years.

Sociology gained its reputation in this country in the 1950s from its supposed ability to shed light upon the social problems around us. It seemed to be claiming that it could find answers because it provided an objective approach to problems which had been, in the past, only understood subjectively, by the individuals and groups in the middle of them. Many sociologists seemed to promise more than this even; they seemed to be saying that they could point to solutions to these problems which society could follow. As the 1950s became the 1960s the scope of sociology seemed widened until it covered every aspect of our experience of life. It grew especially in the fields of education and deviance, and I was a child of those two particular growths.

By the end of the 1960s, though, it became obvious that it was not coming up with the goods. Its analyses were obscure; its language was odder than ever; its solutions seemed to bear no relationship with the experiences of ordinary people; its objectivity seemed tarnished. This its own boundaries. It has become more and more interested in theory, in its own methodology and, finally and endlessly, in the sociology of sociology.

The social problems that sociology was meant to be helping to solve have remained and have become even more intractable; people are *more* worried and confused about society in 1977 than in 1957; in fact sociology seems to have merely created yet another level of mystification to obscure reality from ordinary people.

So why is this book any different? I think there are two main differences in this work from some of the others. Firstly, there is a bit more clarity in the relationship between intellectual work and its limitations and the political work that is necessary for transforming those social problems. I do not believe that my sociological training provides me with any form of second sight into the 'real nature' of social problems; it also does not provide me with any form of platform to change those problems. What it provides me with is the time to try and understand parts of the world in great detail, and a little training in looking at other people's work in understanding the world. During this time, especially while I was working for this book and in contact with working-class male youth, I had the time to relate the social experiences of these youths to Marxism as a political philosophy. This was not the philosophy that 'sociology' taught me; rather it was one that the kids in Sunderland pointed me towards. How this happens is in part what the book is about. So I claim no special professional skills as a sociologist. Indeed, I suspect that many of the 'profession' won't like this book at all. The second difference of this work is the way in which it is organised. I do not put forward a hypothesis about youth and education, then go out and test it and finally show the results of the testing; I don't do this because my research did not happen this way. I went to start my research with one view of education and left with another; the evidence contained in the middle of that process of change in outlook comes mainly from a group of 14- to 15-year-old boys in Sunderland. Each chapter is organised around a question and each question is answered in one way at the beginning of the chapter and then in a different way at the end. What this portrays is the actual *process* of sociological research. At the end of this book I hope the reader will know a bit more not only about education and working-class male youth, but also about the way in which research is actually carried out.

Yet at every stage the more important of these two aims is to try and discuss the nature of education and youth in the 1970s in the

United Kingdom. This is obviously more important than writing about the way in which sociology is carried out; yet at all times I must stress that the solution to the problems outlined in this book do *not* come from intellectuals and from academics but from political and social action. The ideas and insights that come from this book can merely inform this process – they cannot act as a political programme. For example, my research in this book is mainly about young men at school and on the streets; this does not provide an all-round picture of the problems of education and law in the United Kingdom. It does provide a glimpse of one side of some of the educational problems of a capitalist society. In the last chapter of the book I put these into the context of the politics of education in the United Kingdom. It is within these politics that the solution lies; indeed, since I have carried out this research the whole political nature of the education system has been considered by the Prime Minister in a series of discussions about what the State is doing with education. The last chapter is my own contribution to that debate based upon my reading of the boys in Sunderland; it will try and pose the boys' experience not only within education but within their experience of a class-divided society.

1
Why bother to do research?

To provide a clear picture of sociology as a way of seeing the world I must set out by explaining the reasons why I chose this research topic. Sociologists seem to claim that they became interested in topics because they read the work of other sociologists. It is true that other people's work has an effect upon the way in which they choose a research problem; but the main set of reasons for choice is to be found in the biography of the researcher. Similarly, the way in which the research is tackled usually reflects the particular stance of the sociologist's past. It is imperative, therefore, that I start this chapter with a brief run-down of some of the aspects of my background which led me to my research. Like everyone who carries out research on education, I went to school. Sociologists seem to find that experience of no significance in approaching education. In retrospect, after I had finished my research I could see a number of points where it greatly affected my approach.

As an 11-year-old from a south London working-class background I felt that I was lucky when I passed the 11-plus and went to a grammar school. In my first term I was fairly afraid of the institution, worked as best I could, and managed to come top. During the term, however, we were all asked if we wanted to see the school play, *Othello*. We were told to go home and see if our family wanted to go. My mum and dad had something on that night; I didn't care for Shakespeare and I didn't buy any tickets. I was one of a very small minority, and at the end of the school term was told, not that I had done well, but that I must support the school more. I didn't understand that very well then; it puzzled me because I thought school was about academic subjects. The rest of my time at school was similarly affected by a whole series of events which I could not fathom. My parents assured me that these didn't matter; but it was as if there were unwritten goals and rules which I did not comprehend. Such rules governed a whole range of social behaviour at school; many of my friends were in a similar position and slowly dropped away from the intellectual side of the school.

I went to the London School of Economics and studied sociology and social administration. Whilst there, I took part (along with about 75 per cent of the students) in the 'troubles' of that institution; and again in retrospect there was also a series of unwritten rules about 'academic' behaviour which seemed a mystery. What I did learn there academically was a range of sociological interests which had a practical orientation. Most of the individuals from my degree course went into the more practical sides of social understanding; very few ended up doing theoretical research. I decided that I wanted to carry out a research project for a postgraduate degree, and became interested in the relationship between delinquent behaviour and secondary education. It seemed that previous research had high-lighted the fact that the peak age of delinquent activity seemed always to coincide with the last compulsory year at school. If the school-leaving age was 14, then the age when most delinquent activity took place seemed to be 13; when the school-leaving age went up to 15, the peak age went to 14. It would be a short-odds favourite for any sociologically prophetic punter to put money on the peak age going up to 15 now that the school-leaving age has been raised.

It was this relationship which intrigued me: why should these boys tend to commit more delinquency? Is it the frustrations of school, or what? At this period in the development of sociology a great deal of attention was being paid to deviant activity and a whole range of theories had grown up around the relationship of group youth activity with rule-breaking. My degree at the L. S. E. pushed my interests in the relationship between these theories and the in-stitutional progression of 'the school'.

I went to Durham University to carry out this research because one of the best British sociologists of deviance, Stan Cohen, was lecturing there. I worked with him over the next three years on the research. When I reached Stan Cohen I had a very specific view of how research should be carried out; he, and the boys from Sunderland, assisted me in changing this view of how to do research.

Sociological research – as she has been written

The process of doing sociological research has been written about in many different ways. Each undergraduate and postgraduate degree in sociology has a distinct course in research methods which describes in a structured way the techniques that sociologists use in their attempt to gain some grasp of reality. It is thought important that most of these techniques are taught and written about in ways which separate them from the ways in which 'ordinary' people think. I will try and show the ways in which 'doing sociological research' is just a method of making sense of the world; as well as the fact that 'doing research' changes the way in which the researcher sees the world; a different way of understanding emerges from the research.

However, given the way in which most sociological research has been written up these changes do not come across very clearly. In the past, even if it has been possible for the layman to cut his way through the language of the sociologists, he has been presented with a simplistic layout of the way in which the research took place. The three usual splits in this process have been the hypothesis, theory and methodology, and results and conclusions. Each area is in its own compartment, concerned with its own part of the process. The layman has turned from the mystified versions of theory and the odd simplifications of sociological method and has been interested only in the results provided. He has then seen these results as generated by a 'scientific' process devoid of values, and consummately uninteresting. Consequently, the *method* by which sociological results are produced has remained of interest only to sociologists; it is *their* science, with *their* language. Just as the lorry-driver leaves mechanical physics to the physicists and just drives his truck, so has the teacher, for example, left sociological methodology to the sociologist and got on with trying to understand his or her job.

This has meant that in talking to teachers, social workers and shop stewards I have met an almost universal hostility towards sociologists as the new priests of the 1970s. This hostility correctly identifies this sort of sociology as of no use to real people in the real world. It *can* be of no use to people in the world of production precisely because it has tried to pretend that the way in which it makes sense of the world is qualitatively and professionally very different from the way in which the teacher or the trade unionist makes sense of the world. As a result sociology is now reaping the consequences of *deliberately* alienating itself from the rest of the population.

For example, when a shop steward wants to find out a bit more about the authority structure of his industry, he doesn't go through the highly structured process of hypothesis, theory, method and results; he sets about looking at the factory using the knowledge that he has already. In doing so he may well come across a new set of factors which will completely change his ideas. (For example, he may well discover that all the foremen who seem to be getting promotion are those who are learning golf at the club where his managers play.) He will then follow up these new leads, moving, if necessary, away from his original viewpoint. Therefore his method of research is based upon each new factor that he discovers affecting his ideas and making him look at his factory in a different way. If he were to turn to industrial sociology to assist him he would discover a way of understanding factories, not only written in the most opaque language, but deliberately structured to ensure that each new piece of knowledge does *not* change the original hypothesis. It is written and worked out in such a way as to distance itself from the way in which our shop steward thinks.

As a consequence, of course, hardly any shop steward does look to industrial sociology, for he experiences it as alien. Not only does he ignore the ways of thinking involved, but increasingly he ignores the 'results' that are turned out from this structured sausage-machine. The results are ignored because they are experienced as alienated pieces of knowledge which simply appear out of the blue from the preceding mumbo-jumbo. In this way sociology has come to be seen as apart and impractical; as consisting of ideas that interest and inform only other sociologists or the powerful makers of social policy.

In departing from this I hope to show that social scientific analysis can be of importance to the lay person in assisting his political understanding. In no way can it replace this understanding, but it can make some form of contribution towards it. In this case social scientific research is much too important to be left to the sociologists and makers of social policy. It must start being something which is open to people and to all forms of organisation in helping them to make sense of their world. As such this book takes as its starting point the problems of secondary education as experienced by bored 15-year-old working-class boys, and by tired exasperated teachers.

Doing research

I started my research with a fairly typical social democratic view of educational problems. Whilst there was nothing in these views which 'blamed' the boys involved, there was a general optimism that all these problems were soluble via some form of social engineering. This view of the world affected my whole approach to the research; the problems that I was looking at were caused by mistakes in the system of education and law; overall the system was actually working and was there primarily to assist the individuals in it to gain a better understanding of the world. Obviously there were aspects of this interaction which needed changing; obviously it was not good that many kids were bored, that many of them carried out acts of delinquency or vandalism. But this was caused neither by their failure nor by that of the school. What I was interested in was uncovering those aspects of this relationship that were faulty and seeing how they could be changed.

Having decided to study working-class boys at school and their delinquent behaviour it became important to decide on three questions. Where should the schools be? What sort of schools should they be? How should I get my information? Most obviously I was restricted to an area within easy reach of Durham University. I also wanted to study a fairly homogeneous working-class area in an urban environment. Consequently, I chose Sunderland — on the coast about 18 miles from Durham.

It is impossible to provide the reader with a picture of Sunderland in a hundred thousand words, let alone a few hundred. But a typical pen-picture quotation comes from a book about Sunderland published in 1969.

> Sunderland is a town which is living on the dwindling fat of its Victorian expansion. The legacy of the industrial revolution is apparent in its appearance, its physical structure, its population growth and in a host of social and economic characteristics. Even attitudes are coloured by its past heritage. The depression years, the final death spasm of the 19th century, are still a real memory amongst much of the town's population and impinge upon the attitudes of the working population. This imprint of the past, rooted in a continuing dependence on heavy industry, is found to a much greater degree than in the towns of the Midlands or even Lancashire, since the spread of light manufacturing has had only marginal effects in the North—East. [1]

The problem of doing research in any one place and then generalising over a wider area is typified by this piece of research.

Sunderland is by no means 'typical' of the towns of the United Kingdom, but then neither are London, Leicester, Glasgow, Chester or Belfast. The typical town does not exist to be studied; instead we must try and draw some of the conclusions that we can, whilst all the time being aware that, for example, the average wage in Sunderland is considerably lower than in Coventry, and that Sunderland is over 200 miles from London and a bit off the beaten track as far as pop tours are concerned as well as a host of other factors. In drawing the conclusion in the book I will return to this point.

Having mentioned the fact that I chose Sunderland for my research, two points are important to make. Firstly, in order to gain the confidence of institutions and individuals it is vital for any person attempting to communicate to a wider audience to change all the names and possible identifications. Therefore the boys' names, teachers' names and names of places have all been changed; this may prove a minor irritant to those individuals who would like to be able to trace and check what I have written. For this I apologise. I would ask all individuals who feel so aggrieved to ask themselves how they would feel about the publication of their thoughts about their employer. Secondly, a word about doing research in a place like Sunderland. In getting to know the north-east, I found a fiercely regionally partisan place. Many people in that town may well feel that I was a carpet-bagger, simply criticising the work of their institutions, portraying a picture of their kids, calling their place a Smash Street area. There is, of course, some validity in the charge of carpet-bagging; I don't come from Sunderland, I don't live there now; I went there to do research, and only really for that purpose. This is the wrong way to go about things, but as a Ph.D. student and one of the academic gypsies who move around the country I felt that I had little choice about where I 'settled'. In fact it depended upon where I could find suitable supervision and where I could get a grant. Therefore what I have got to say below does NOT relate purely to Sunderland; the schools, police and youth of Sunderland are not, in *respect of this piece of writing*, very different from those of London or Coventry. People of the north-east have become very touchy about outsiders criticising them; I don't want to be seen to be doing that in any way.

The two areas of Sunderland that contain the two schools in which I worked need a brief introduction. Tavistock council estate, which contains Municipal Comprehensive School, is a large post-Second World War estate upon the outskirts of Sunderland, like (and a bit unlike) a hundred others throughout the country on the fringes of conurbations. The estate is totally of council houses, built around a service area of shops. The area immediately strikes you as working class if you have any conception of the hierarchy of the society within which we live.

On the other hand, everyone would have agreed that Municipal Comprehensive School was one of the best and newest secondary schools in the country. It had a headmaster not unknown as an educationalist and the staff had been hand-picked by him. He told me that he felt that the catchment area for the school had been especially designed to include only council houses. Despite this homogeneity in its pupils, I would believe that, physically, Municipal Comprehensive School was one of the best in the country.

The area where Cunningham Secondary School was situated was very different. This was an older area — late-Victorian — with most of the housing stuck between a main road and beside the sea. Whilst being very different from the Tavistock estate, it did, similarly, compel the observer to label it working class. The school was very different. Cramped in poor conditions, a typical school-board school with high, Victorian, poorly-lit rooms. A noisy class in this school could be heard through half the school. The headmaster had a very different idea about postgraduates coming in and doing research in his school, and I found it impossible to get to know this school so well. Consequently this was to change the emphasis of the research a little.

Importantly, I knew a teacher at Municipal Comprehensive and someone who had taught at Cunningham. Both of them helped me a great deal with background information throughout the research. They were obviously a factor in making this choice of schools, but the most important factor was the apparent excellence of Municipal Comprehensive. If I wanted to find out some of the unintended consequences of secondary education in the field of deviant behaviour, I had to select a school for the main piece of the research that could not be dismissed as one of the worst 10 per cent in the country. In selecting Cunningham I was selecting a school which was totally different in a physical and educational sense; this was not done simply so that I could compare a 'good' school and a 'bad' school and their effect on the children; rather I wanted two different sets of social relationships. What is amazing is that with the exception of one area — that is, pop music — the boys experienced BOTH these schools in exactly the same way. This would back up the famous quotation at the start of the Newsom Report:

Headmaster (to pupil who is just leaving, pointing to the new school buildings): 'Well, what do you think of the new school now then?'

Boy: 'You can build it out of marble but it would still be a bloody school.'[2]

Choosing research methods within a school

There are a number of ways in which I could have gone about getting information about the boys' experience. The following are the two that I chose from.

Teaching in a school — filling a role

Research in most areas of society is best carried out where the researcher can fit into the institutions as unobtrusively as possible. Importantly though, as far as the school is concerned, there is only one major participant role open to the adult researcher — that of teacher. If you want to gather information about any area of social life the choice is between trying to live it yourself and collecting material as you go along, and being something special in the situation and gathering the ideas and information that come to you because you are something special. If, in researching into school, you accept the role of being a teacher as the way to gain information, it shows that you feel that it is possible to get information from the pupils and still be a teacher.

Hargreaves writes about his research technique:

The writer spent a complete year in the school. For the first two terms he was present for the whole school day. He taught all the fourth year boys at some stage, as well as other year-groups; he observed the pupils in lessons conducted by all the teachers; he administered questionnaires and conducted interviews; he used every available opportunity for informal discussion with the boys; he accompanied them on some official school visits and holidays; he joined them in some of their out-of-school activities. In a word the researcher entered the school as a participant observer, armed with his own training and teaching experience and with the intention of examining the behaviour and attitudes of boys in the school and their relationship with the teachers and with one another.[3]

Acting as a teacher, then, gives Hargreaves an opening to a tremendous amount of information, yet I felt this would not serve my purposes. Those readers who are teachers and those who remember their schooldays will be aware, I hope, of the impossibility of actually gaining accurate information from pupils if you *are* a teacher. Being labelled as such breaks the possibility of gaining certain sorts of information at all. What happens if a pupil smokes? What happens if he really hates one of your colleagues? What happens if he knows that a boy is going to try and burn down a section of the school? All of these pieces of information are differently available from the kids to individuals who are labelled as teachers and to others. Personally I felt that the gap between teacher and taught would preclude me from obtaining some of the more sensitive information about the boys which I felt was essential. So I decided not to teach.

An alternative role – the cockney writer

However, as Hargreaves points out, 'Any adult [who is not dressed as a workman] appearing in school must in their [the pupils'] eyes, have some strong connection with the teaching profession.'[4] Consequently it became important as soon as possible to sever the connection that must exist in the boys' eyes between the teaching profession and myself.

This meant that the research and the whole of this book are about the boys at school and not about the teachers of that school. It was impossible to get at the information about the boys if you were seen talking to teachers too often; I had to make an early choice in the school and did so in favour of learning more about the boys' situation.

However, it was not sufficient simply to decide not to be a teacher; it became important to create a role for myself which was not threatening. This was equally true of the teachers, since they, together with the headmaster, could have decided to stop my research whenever they felt it threaten them; equally, if they had accepted me with open arms it would have meant that the boys would not be likely to trust me greatly. Creating this ambiguity in the teachers' minds was not a difficult strategy to adopt since in the first place I had no clear idea of the precise nature of my research. This meant that when asked what I was doing, I generally replied in a fairly rambling way. Secondly, I was fairly scared of the teachers. Entering a school staffroom as a stranger is not the easiest social situation to feel at home in.

Consequently, it was by choice as much as design that I spent most lunch-hours with the kids.

Nevertheless, the importance of being at least partially accepted by the teachers, whilst also being totally accepted by the boys, left me with a number of mundane problems to confront. How long should my hair be to persuade the boys that I wasn't a student teacher at heart? How short should my hair be to get me into the school? Similarly with dress. And most importantly with behaviour. In most south of England schools my south London working-class accent would have O. K.'d me with the boys; but, given a well-founded northern distrust of anyone south of Teesside as incipient 'southern cream-puffs', this would not work here. Over time though, my Londonness assisted me in getting through to the kids, since they were interested in such places as West Ham, Millwall and the Kings Road.

All of this would have been to no avail, though, unless I could create in the boys' minds a role for me that didn't threaten them. The role of writer, of someone writing a book about them, was the truest one; I said I was only interested in them; that *they* were the reason that I was at the school; that I wanted them to say the things the way they wanted, using their language, and I didn't care about spelling, or grammar, or talking proper. This had an important effect since I was in their minds Paul Corrigan who was writing a book about them, and also I was actually interested in *their* words and ideas. The only come-back I had from this was a feeling that since they were doing the work (talking) and I was getting paid for the book, I should give them a cut.

Methods used to get information about the boys' experiences

At this stage I would hope that the reaction of many of the ladies reading the book is fairly irate about my failure to mention girls at all to date. Throughout, this book follows the male-dominated socio-logical line of researching only into male adolescent activity; male delinquency; male experience of school. There is little real defence of this total exclusion of half of the population from sociological research; my only defence is that I was going to have to use a lot of the insights gained from my own adolescent experience. The one thing which feminists would allow in my defence was my own recognition of the different problems of adolescent behaviour experienced by girls; they suffer a series of multiple oppressions which are beyond my experience and, like being adolescent in a black ghetto, need researching and writing about by someone who has experienced those oppressions, so I was restricted to the problems of working-class MALE adolescent experience of school.

Another important personal failure which changes the research techniques a lot is the fact that I am 6ft 4in tall and that most 14-year-olds in Sunderland are considerably smaller than that. This means that the sort of unobtrusive participant observation by hanging around on a corner with them was simply impossible. Rather, it would have consisted of a totally different situation where the 'Tavistock boys' had suddenly picked up this large ally to use in street fights: the existence of this large ally would have grossly changed their actions.

So, neither inside or outside the school was it possible for me to use the best method of gaining information. I had to use alternative techniques.

The questionnaire

In asking the boys to answer a questionnaire I realised that I was doing something far from original. Yet there were sets of background information about the boys' experiences which could only really be gained by this method. I needed some information before I could use the more sensitive techniques of structured interview, observation and just plain chatting. So I administered a questionnaire myself to groups of boys in both schools.

I gave the questionnaires to 48 boys from Municipal School and 45 from Cunningham. I asked the headmasters to provide me with boys who were most probably leaving that year. (Since the school-leaving age had not at the time been raised, this meant that they were all nearly 15.) In answer to all the other more specific questions from the headmasters I simply answered that I wanted a 'cross-section'. Both said that the boys that they selected represented their year quite well; both warned me that there were several terrors and horrors in the group; both said that there were some 'good lads' in it.

I gave the questionnaires to the boys, preceded by a patter which I hoped would allay some of their fears. There were a variety of techniques used in the questionnaire, but in the pilot survey and throughout I realised the tremendous difficulty of collecting information from people whose thoughts are not expressed in the same way as the researcher's. Many of the boys found difficulty in writing at all, and a few of them just didn't write anything or answer any questions. All the time I stressed that I did not mind if they didn't write sentences and that one word would do in sentence completion. Overall the questionnaire tried to get round this as much as possible by providing a spread of different methods of articulation. Importantly, too, I gave out the questionnaires to *groups* of boys, giving them much more confidence since they were filling them in with their mates.

The interview

I interviewed all the boys in Municipal School that I had given the questionnaire to. It is important to stress why I didn't interview any of the boys from Cunningham School as it says a lot about the way in which sociological research *actually happens* (rather than the way in which sociologists write about their research). The headmaster of Cunningham School was not too pleased at the thought of me going to his school two or three times a week with my tape recorder and could well have stopped me interviewing half-way through. Therefore, since the interviews were to be supplemented by general observations about the way in which the school worked, I thought it might be better to concentrate on getting to know the social relationships involved with one school. At the same time, in analysing the two schools' answers to my questions, I discovered no significant difference between the responses of the two sets of boys. This was surprising, since from the outside the schools appeared so different; but in another way it was not surprising at all, since the whole message that the research ends up saying is that school is school for these boys, and it is the structure of perceived compulsion that makes it such an oppressive experience.

Other methods

Apart from the questionnaires and interviews there were other ways of obtaining information which were used throughout my research. It is these that are generally forgotten when sociologists write up their research. Most importantly as far as the understanding of these schools is concerned, I spent a lot of time just in the school, looking, trying to understand the way in which structures worked. This provided me with insights which made a lot of the interpretation of the other data possible. It directed my reading in certain directions. I also spent some time just chatting to boys at lunchtimes; in these situations the research process is seen as a two-way process. They were making sense of my world as much as I was making sense of theirs. They asked about drugs, student demonstrations, politics, sex, pop music, football, south of Teesside, and all the other things which are so very odd to them. Towards the end of the research they could have written a fairly good report on what it is like for a working-class postgraduate to live in a fairly bourgeois town (Durham) but do research in a working-class area of a city. But of course these boys at the end of the research go down the pits or into the Navy. THEY don't get to write the books.

Getting to know these boys in this way allowed me some greater understanding of their school experiences. It also directed my research and my methods in a different way. It forced me to look at the educational system of this country historically in order to try and find out why these boys had to go to school. Thus one of the methods of investigation became the use of the historical method.

Conclusion

What this chapter has tried to do is show the similarity between the sociological methods that I used to try to make sense of a problem I was interested in, and the ways in which ordinary people make sense of their world. It may appear a mess and imprecise; yet I believe that it represents much more fully the real way in which an analysis of a situation makes sense of the world for people. Whether sociology is a science, a craft or a philosophy, it is nothing if it fails to discuss the experienced problems of ordinary people; and it is nothing if it fails to do this in a way which people can understand.

Therefore in the following five chapters I have arranged my research around five questions which I consider of social importance. At the beginning of each chapter I have outlined one sort of answer to the question – the answer with which I entered my research. Then I use large chunks of the kids' words about their worlds to try and supply another answer to the question. The distance between these two answers does, I think, measure the distance between sociology and the experienced world. Thirdly, I try to follow some of the leads that the boys' words had given me in terms of other areas of research. Fourthly, I provide a very different sort of answer to the question that the chapter is based upon. The result may appear less structured than most sociological research, yet it will provide the reader with a view of what it is like to do research; and what it is like to learn and change one's opinions and ideas whilst doing it. I think the research answers some questions and asks a lot of others; overall it shows the vital importance of actually getting down to trying to understand the real world and not taking the obvious answers as the right ones.

You can't solve a problem? Well get down and investigate the present facts and the past history! When you have investigated a problem, you will know how to solve it. Only a blockhead cudgels his brains on his own or together with a group to 'find a solution' or 'evolve an idea' without making an investigation. It must be stressed that this cannot possibly lead to any effective solution or to any good ideas. [5]

2
Why do kids play truant?

Why should I start by looking at truancy? After all, the great majority of kids spend the great majority of their time at school safely in their classrooms. They mostly do *go* to school, even if they don't behave. Yet there are at least two reasons for looking at truancy as a separate category of behaviour.

Firstly, the boys themselves quickly told me that *their* main problem was going to school. It may seem farcical but it did appear that school might not be so bad if you did not HAVE to go. Therefore *having* to go to school – in effect the reverse of truancy, but also its major cause – was where the boys started off their everyday school experiences. It seemed correct to start off my own analysis there also.

Secondly, truancy has become one of the most discussed 'problems' in the educational world. The Department of Education and Science does not collect any index of truancy, so it is not possible to provide a nice simple graph showing increase or decrease over the past twenty years. In any case, one of the main points of this chapter is to point out the uselessness of any statistics that would be collected. There is no point in adding up ticks in registers and believing that they represent boys in classrooms, then looking at the crosses and saying that x per cent of the crosses are truants. Anyone who can remember school knows the true relationship between registration and attendance. The phrase in the north-east is 'dolling off', in Coventry it's 'wagging it'; it means the same thing: skipping the classes that you want to miss.

My initial perceptions of education

I went into the research with a view of education which could loosely be called the liberal social-democratic view. I thought education was a Good Thing; I believed that the more of It there was about the better; that everyone should have as much of It as possible; that It did everyone good. It is within this belief that the majority of educational discussion takes place. It has been seen as a cure for all sorts of collective and individual troubles over the past 150 years. It has been suggested as a policy to cure juvenile crime, lack of respect for authority, industrial unrest, soccer hooliganism, and all other behavioural problems that are felt to confront working-class kids. This treatment has been suggested in increasing doses, starting at earlier ages and finishing at later ages. The strength of the dose and slight changes in the ingredients have been continually tried; but the major ideology that it sees itself as a curative for evils is still one of the main parameters of educational thinking.

The second major factor in common-sense educational ideas is that education is an attempt to transfer bodies of ideas from one group of society to another, more ignorant, group in society. This in itself is viewed as axiomatic, and also part of the 'goodness' of education.

These two ideas are so widely held by those in the educational establishment that, up until a few years ago, it would have been madness to suggest anything to the contrary. Given the totality of this as an ideology, those people that researched into the ways in which working-class boys made sense of education expected that the boys themselves would see education as a good thing and as a transfer of knowledge to them. Researchers including myself did believe that working-class boys had this view of education; we felt that they valued education and held to the values of the educational in-stitutions. However, we were all confronted with the problem that the boys did not behave in accordance with these values. Boys played truant, acted as if they hated education, generally mucked about in school; they did all this in spite of the fact that they, like everyone else in society, felt that education was doing them good.

This paradox provides, both in the field of education and in the field of social behaviour generally, a whole sub-discipline of soci-ology with its *raison d'être*. The sociology of deviance would mean very little without the need to explain why people seem continually to act in ways that do not relate to society's values. Immediately, the common-sense answer, and the answer provided within the sociology of deviance, is that people who act in this way should change their values.

Deviancy theory has tried to explain the phenomenon of classroom misbehaviour by seeing the process as one where boys along with everyone else perceive education as valuable, and try to attain certain values that the school encourages. Thus they become ambitious; they try to learn; they try to plan ahead; they try to see the wider implications of the world that they live in and to understand them in educational terms. In short they try to use the educational system to increase their knowledge of the world, and they try to change their behaviour to fit in with this system.

However, this argument continues, the education system does not provide these boys with the opportunities for attaining these values. The education system does not allow sufficient mobility for working-class children. It consists of a series of increasingly difficult hurdles which are raised against them. These hurdles have never been correctly overcome despite continuous attempts at reform, through-out this century. They have failed to realise the differential effects that home background has on different groups of pupils. Thus some kids come from homes which are bereft of books, with parents who fail to appreciate the importance of education for their children's success in life; in short they come from 'educationally disadvantaged' homes.

I will develop this part of the model later on; for the moment, though, it is sufficient to say that the interaction between school and home ensures that school, for most working-class boys, does not allow them to act in tune with these new values that they have learnt. So that, in this argument, this becomes the crucial problem for working-class kids. They have inculcated middle-class values through the medium of school, and are trying to attain the type of life commensurate with these values; but the school itself, in failing to interact fully with their homes, does not allow them to behave that way – there are structural blocks which stop them from attaining this life style. This problem for these boys means that they are under a great deal of psychological tension; they hold values which are unattainable; they are, for example, ambitious yet have no chance of getting on in the world since they cannot use the education system as a ladder. This psychological tension resolves itself in what has been called 'negative formation'.[1] Negative formation solves the problem by turning the values of the school upon their heads and bringing them in line with the boys' behaviour. Thus if the boys cannot be ambitious because the structure of education does not allow them to be, then they become deliberately unambitious. For the first time now they have a set of values which are in line with their own behaviour, thereby solving their tensions.

But the solution of the boys' problems, in this way, is not an *individual* solution. It takes place in a group situation where there are many other boys in a similar state. Consequently, the formation of values to fit their behaviour takes place within a group of boys all of whom were 'failing'. This 'sub-culture' within the school reinforces itself by recognising that its own problems are not simply individual, but that they are being suffered by certain sorts of boys. Thus, for example, the rougher boys find that they all have similar sorts of problems in this area and they tend to find their solutions together. In this way groups of boys are formed whose values are diametrically opposed to those of the school; diametrically opposed because they have tried and failed to attain the school's values.

These deviancy theories became transferred to the sociology of education in the late 1960s, typified in such work as that of Hargreaves.[2] They also became part of educational policy at about that time; it was thought vital to try to stop the negative formation of anti-school values, to try to introduce the boys to things that interested them; to change the curriculum to education relevant to working-class children. The mode III form of C. S. E. examination was created to try to provide the room for manoeuvre where this could occur. Social studies courses and courses in 'citizenship' became part of the secondary school curricula. All of these were basically designed to attempt to help make the kids come to terms with the institutions that they went to. Admittedly the institutions were to be changed, but never fundamentally. The boys and girls were to have their consent to education won by a number of concessions in the running of the school, and in the subjects taught.

Despite these changes, though, it still appeared that kids disliked school; they didn't like it when it was all maths and exams; they now didn't seem to like it when it was all civics and projects. In this way, I was provided with my research problem. I believed that it would be possible, using a mixture of the deviancy theories I have discussed, to try to explain why the boys failed to come to terms with that traditional home–school clash documented in the educationists of the 1950s and the policies of the 1960s. Perhaps it would be in terms of the ways in which boys formed themselves into groups of disadvantaged; and then formed anti-school groups on the model of juvenile gangs. The formation of these groups would then be the vital process to understand. It was within the field of group-formation that I expected to find the answer; the ways in which the negative formation of values led to a group disassociation from the school. This group then became the problem for the school to cope with.

This explanation appealed to me in terms of my autobiography since it did not wholly *blame* the boys; rather it said that they were not equipped to come to terms with the school's demands, and that this led them to form oppositional groups. What the boys thought was a bit different altogether.

What the boys think about school

In talking to the boys with the above model in mind I expected to find people truanting because they saw it as a 'good' thing. However, in one the most significant attitudes that the boys expressed, a very different rationale emerged.

I asked the boys to complete the sentence 'I come to school because . . .' and the answers were grouped as follows:

Compulsion	52	(It's the law; I have to; me Mum would get put in prison)
Muck teacher about	13	(To have a laugh with the teacher)
To learn	18	(To do my lessons)
It is good	5	(It's good; I enjoy it)
No answer	5	

In a complex way the nature of this answer gives us clues to two sets of ideas: 50 of the boys perceive school as a place that you only go to because you HAVE to; and it provides us with answers expressed not at all in terms of values, but in terms of power.

So what does this compulsion mean to the boys? To understand their reactions to it we must look at working-class cultural reactions to authority when it impinges upon their daily lives.

In a book which seems to be one long finger-wagging exercise at the working-class child, Klein notes that working-class attitudes to authority are shaped by their experiences at home with their parents. Here, Klein says, they learn only one rule of behaviour that is strongly enforced:

> steer clear of trouble, give in to a stronger force. On the street, as in the home, there is a constant aggressively hinged excitement. Parents shout at neighbours and at their children. When they can get away with it, their children shout back. Adults cuff or thrash children, who will do the same to those who are weaker than themselves. Through it all the Mother is constantly talking at the

child issuing orders that are not carried out. All this adds to the unreliability of the environment. The inconsistent treatment confirms the child's general experience of life. What the child does may at one time be smiled at indulgently or even proudly, and at another time be greeted with a shout or a blow. This kind of do-as-you-like indulgence gives the home a connotation of refuge, of safety from the demands of the outside world. Like any other child he is homesick and pleased when he does not have to go to school. Put in this particular case the home is a refuge from demands which if they are inescapable and must be met, shape the personality to be well-adjusted to modern civilised standards of living. If they find a situation disturbing or unpleasant they give the easy, obvious, quick response if there is one, or they quickly reject the whole situation. [3]

The obviously class-biased tone of the book comes over in this quotation; the lack of any questioning of 'modern civilised standards of living'; the underlying belief in controlling behaviour through some moral system; they all betray a jaundiced view of these kids' actions. However, one thing that comes across in this and other studies of working-class culture is that the kids learn a specific way of dealing with authority. There seem to be three major stages in this process: firstly, to ignore it and it may well go away (like Dad's temper); secondly, to try and remove yourself from it as much as possible; thirdly, to recognise it only as far as it can enforce recognition.

If we explore alternative models of coping with authority, there are two of significance which never feature in any writing about working-class culture. Firstly, it is possible to refuse to recognise the authority despite its power. In other words, to make a moral stand against something which is felt to be wrong; to carry out a set of actions despite the fact that the power ranged against you is great. This idealistic refusal seems to have no part in working-class culture. In studies of truancy, we have little evidence of boys deliberately walking out of school in view of the headmaster in order to make their point against the system.

Secondly, working-class culture does not comply, or fail to comply, with 'authority' because of a set of closely worked out moral precepts. Indeed, all the writers stress the impossibility, in the environment of a working-class family, of learning to comply with a set of prescriptions. Instead they all comment on the lack of a moral set of rules by showing the ways in which middle-class morality is not complied with.

Both of these attitudes to authority are linked with the common-sense view of truancy outlined at the beginning of the chapter, since they discuss the ways in which individuals control their action through sets of values; or, in terms of our explanation of truancy, deliberately flaunt authority. If we now look back at the boys' answers on page 22 we can see how they back up the writings on working-class culture, showing a significant lack of behaviour linked only to middle-class values but devoid of power.

It is possible to envisage a different response to truancy from a group with a different set of cultural experiences. For example, if a university lecturer whose students didn't attend his lectures because they found them of no consequence made his lectures compulsory, the students would be likely to try and persuade him to change his mind. Further, they would argue with him around such ideas as freedom and choice, and if that failed they would try and apply collective political pressure in the form of petitions, pressure from their student unions, and interviews with their professor. If all else failed they would then organise a collective boycott, with pickets, leaflets and so on. These sets of options may be obvious to us, and we may use them when we come against a form of authority with which we disagree. They are not, though, open to working-class boys at school since they in no way relate to their background experience.

The exact nature of truancy as a solution to problems of compulsory attendance is a complex one. For, by the age of 14, a number of crucial lessons *have* been learnt by the boys at school, though these may have little to do with the content of history or geography books. Most obviously the power behind the compulsory nature of schooling is very visible to the boys. Of the several questions asked about truancy in the questionnaire and in the interview, the importance of the sanction was constantly mentioned by the boys, whereas only a few commented on the rightness or wrongness of truancy. The major restraint upon increased truancy therefore was a recognition of power rather than a moral compliance.

Suppose a close friend	Yes	28
of yours was thinking of playing	No	64
truant, would you try and talk him	No answer	2
out of it?		

Why is that?	It is bad	6
	Get into trouble	22
	It's up to him	47
	I'd go with him	13
	No answer	5

Therefore when we look at the reasons why 28 boys would try and persuade their friend not to play truant we find only six that mentioned a moral reason:

'Because it is a bad thing to do' — *Humph*
'It's not right' — *Bill*
'Because it's very wrong to play truant' — *Phil*

With all the others there was a very shrewd perception of the power of the state over their choice about going to school. They seemed to know this power both in extent and in its particular consequences:

'I would never do it because in the end they nearly always get caught' — *Jimmy*
'Because he might get into serious trouble if he was caught' — *Derek M.*

All these answers betray a knowledge of the extent of the power ranged against them. The specifics of this power both inside and outside the school were outlined by other boys:

'Because if you do when you get back you will be caned and you will get a black mark' — *Pete*
'It's none of my business [to stop him]. It's the School Board man's job' — *Chas*

and more specifically:

'Because he might get caught and then he might have to go to court' — *Bob*

The boys also spelt out what would happen in court:

'Because he would be put away and not get a job at all' — *Harry*
'To stop him from getting himself put into a home' — *Mike*

So within the frame of reference of the boys all these powerful forces are ranged against him. Thus when a boy says that he will try and persuade his friend not to play truant we should in no sense take it as agreement with school values. Similarly, there is no mention of truancy as a specific attempt to violate school norms. The relative importance of the activity, the rationale behind it and the evaluation of the sanctions against it can be summed up in Johnny's words: 'Well, the DAY will soon be over, but he could get wronged, and may be put on probation.' This says quite simply that to enforce a rule the sanction must be a more powerful force than the pain of compliance.

Have you played truant in the past year?		
	Never	37
	Once or twice	38
	Several times	5
	Often	9
	No answer	4

Thus the 37 boys above who never played truant do not necessarily agree with or support the major values of the school; they are much more likely to be simply afraid of the consequences of their action. Indeed, since only nine boys said that they played truant often it would seem that this fear of sanction was sufficiently strong to overcome any reason for truanting.

(The boys use the word 'wronged' not to register rights and wrongs but to describe getting into trouble. Thus 'he gets wronged for that' means that he gets into trouble.)

It is here, though, that we come up against our first major difficulty in answering the question that began this chapter. For, while the boys recognise the power of the school to stop truanting, and while this recognition stops them from playing truant, there are alternative methods of not staying at school. The definition of truanting is held both by the boys and by the teachers as staying away from school without a sick note. But what exactly is staying away from school? As far as the teachers are concerned there are two realities. One is that the pupil should be sitting in the classroom for the lessons; the other is that he should be registered at the beginning of the morning and afternoon. The ritual of registration at school provides the authorities with proof of the child's attendance at school. If he is not registered and if he does not produce a sick note, then he is truanting. However, if he is registered, then as far as the authorities are concerned the child is at school.

The reality for the boys, though, is different. Their concern about truanting is based upon their fear of sanctions. Therefore they are keen to get their registration ticks because a tick protects them from the sanctions used against truants. Getting a tick in a book, though, does not necessarily imply attendance at school as far as the *experience* of education is concerned, and the boys have developed methods to negate the effect of attendance at school without activating the sanctions against truancy. Simply, the boys attend registration and do not attend what they find to be the most boring of the lessons. In this way the boys are not strictly playing truant, and as such they would not admit to truancy on a self-report survey that I used. If they skip this lesson and that, they still miss the lessons, and it becomes a matter for the control of the individual teachers rather than taking on the whole panoply of the law. At worst the headmaster is brought into the matter, but never the police, courts or approved schools.

In its mildest form 'dolling off' was outlined by one boy:

Question What do you think about boys that play truant?
Derek Well, there again, it's a boring lesson. I'll give you an instance — there was a lesson with a cookery teacher and it should have been science and we just read about cookery. Every week, she used to say, 'If you behave yourself you would have been out on the grass this week'. Well, that used to be said every week. So boys started to drift out and they got caught and told off.

What is interesting here is the way that non-attendance at this particular lesson is linked with the particular purpose of that particular teacher. The teacher using a deprivation of privilege (going out on the grass) actually to enforce discipline, not only fails to enforce that discipline, but also has the boys taking that particular privilege on their own. This particularistic relationship between the boys missing lessons and the lessons themselves came over again and again in the answers.

Question What do you think about boys that play truant?
Albert I've played truant, it's just because you get so sick of school. In engineering drawing I stopped off because there's this teacher and he is always picking on you and it's hard and I don't know what to do, so I just stay off.

Question Why do you think boys play truant?
Albert It's just like with teachers who are saying things that are too hard to do. They get sick of teachers who are just picking on them and sending them out of the class and that; so they just don't go.

It seems precisely for cases such as this that education was made compulsory. If boys leave whenever they feel like it, or when they feel that the teacher has overstepped the mark, then the whole system is undermined. Yet it seems that boys have hit *exactly* upon the weakness of compulsion by treating each lesson differentially.

Question Why do you doll off?
Dick Well, last Wednesday afternoon, it was because we were getting P. E. and we were getting running and they make you run round the pitches six or seven times, and if you didn't go they caned you and if you cut the corners you'd get hit. Sometimes I haven't got my kit, and some lessons if I haven't done my homework I'll stop off.
Question So it's on specific things?
Dick Yes. I would stop off a lesson if I didn't feel like it.

Stopping off lessons when they feel like it once more seems specifically to negate the purpose of school sanctions. It seemed that it was meant primarily as a form of protection from the rigours of certain lessons; that boys would doll off not in an attempt to attack the school, but rather to keep themselves from attack from the school. This meant that the *initiation* of the problem came from outside the boys.

Truancy — is it a question of values at all?

At this stage of answering the question of 'why boys play truant' the research seemed to reach a very crucial disjuncture. There was a great difference between the sorts of answers that I had anticipated from the boys and the nature of their reality. It was not simply that my original 'research hypothesis' about the rejection of school values was being disproved by my research; rather it was the fact that the whole theory seemed totally *irrelevant* to the boys' experiences. In looking at their own ideas about truancy a number of different themes come across. It does not seem that truancy is an action which is meant to *attack the school values* in any way; rather the action seems to have something to do with the boys' protection of themselves from things that they don't like. Thus there are specific actions against specific lessons where the boys absent themselves. None of the boys mentions the rights and wrongs of such forms of action, rather they seem to be constantly concerned with the POWER of the school and the law in making them (and attempting to make them) attend school as a whole and certain lessons specifically. This difference between my hypothesis expressed in terms of values and the boys' views expressed in terms of actions led me to change the structure of the research completely. This provides a concrete example of the real way in which research is carried out. It would have been very stupid for me to have ploughed on at this point with my original set of ideas about the research.

In this particular case, it was a specially vivid example of the change that can come about, for I not only changed the way I was looking at the research but very practically changed the main area of concern. Admittedly I was still interested in education, in boys' behaviour, and in dolling off school. However, now I was concerned to take the boys' ideas seriously and to see why the power of the state was attempting to make them go to school. This meant that the focus of the research changed from simply being about the boys' perceptions of their situation to seeing their perceptions as the *starting-point* of the research, and therefore looking at the relationship between school refusal and the power of the state in making boys go to school.

The answer to the question 'Why do boys play truant?' became answerable only in relation to the question 'Why are boys made to go to school?'. Compulsory education then becomes explicable only by coming to grips with truancy; the boy who stays off P. E. becomes intelligible only in terms of why the law tries to make him go in the first place.

Why are schools compulsory? What are 'schools'?

In order to understand the compulsory nature of British education it is necessary to come to grips with the nature of the 'education' itself. I have put quotation marks around the word 'school' because the meaning of the word is something that we have all learnt to take for granted. Young[4] sees that education has become one of the 'dominant legitimising categories' in studying social relations. This means that it acts as one of the major means of validating the forms of social relationship that exist at present. All such categories are dominant precisely because the bulk of the population and most intellectuals see them as above debate. They are universally regarded as good or bad things without ever any real questioning as to their specific meaning. In this way education has been one of the continuing 'Good Things' for people since the 1860s. Given this long a run as one of the universally accepted categories of goodness in our society why should I question it in this research? The reasons for questioning it are found in the kids' experiences. They carry out a lot more than a mere intellectual questioning of its worth; from the quotes above they seem to regard it with extreme dislike and *far* from a 'Good Thing'. Therefore it is from the boys' experience of the world that I as an analyst felt it important to question the legitimacy and worth of the category of 'education'.

When I began looking at the history of the concept I quickly discovered that the related set of ideas had not always been taken for granted. The politically neutralised idea had been the subject in the nineteenth century not only of debate and discussion but also of *political struggle*. The traditional view of the creation of a national system of education in England is one that pictures the working class pressurising an unwilling middle class into spending taxation revenues upon educating its children because it could not afford to do so itself. As one of its major sets of characters this picture portrays a group of dedicated social reformers who spend half a century reporting and lobbying Parliament, which is dominated by *laissez-faire*. These individuals are the inspectorate who appear within this orthodoxy to be interested in the good of the society as a whole. They are pictured as differing from the mass of the people only in so far as they are progressives a little ahead of their time in their ideas.

This picture leaves out any struggle at all about the meaning of 'education', assuming that the working class and the middle class agreed on its meaning and only disagreed on the *amount* that it should be applied to the population. I looked at the historical picture with a *very* different perspective of history which concentrated more upon ways in which the different classes of nineteenth-century British society expressed different political positions. This perspective analyses state activity as an attempt to interfere differentially in the lives of different sections of the population.

State education as imposition

All histories agree that the forty years prior to the education Acts of

1870 saw considerable activity in education on the part of the central government, particularly in the field of inspection. This inspection was used both as a direct attempt to create a 'national' system of education and to attack the concept of education that was evolving within the working-class culture of the time. It has been claimed that the setting up of an education system for the working class created this obsession. The nature and language of this obsession is noted in typical fashion in a leader in *The Times* in 1854:

The education of the people has been constantly discussed for many years but the power of the State has been paralysed because education is a subject of 'bitter dispute and animosity'. Church here either regarded all plans for state education as the mainten- ance of some exclusive ecclesiastical domination or as a wicked device for the utter destruction of all religious belief amongst the people generally. Meanwhile the character and the conduct of the people are constantly being formed under the influence of their surroundings. While we are disputing which ought to be con- sidered the most beneficial system of education, we leave the great mass of the people to be influenced and formed by the very worst possible teachers. Certain teachers, indeed, could be called in- structors for evil. The Chartist movement might no longer be the dangerous presage of civil strife denounced by Kay-Shuttleworth in 1839, but in 1850 Harney's *Red Republican* has published in full 'the Communist Manifesto' supporting every revolutionary move- ment against the existing social and political order of things, and calling on working men of all countries to unite; the National Reform League was campaigning for the nationalisation of land, atheism was being actively propagated. In the very heart of the apparently well-ordered community enough evil teaching was going on to startle, if not alarm, the most firm-minded. Systems the most destructive of the peace, the happiness and the virtue of society, are boldly, perseveringly, and without let or hindrance, openly taught and recommended to the acceptance of people with great zeal, if not with great ability. Cheap publications containing the wildest and the most anarchical doctrines are scattered, broadcast over the land, in which religion and morality are perverted and scoffed at, and every rule of conduct which experience has sanctioned, and on which the very existence of society depends, openly assailed. While in their place are sought to be established doctrines as outrageous as the maddest ravings of furious insanity—as wicked as the most devilish spirit could possibly have devised. The middle classes who pass their lives in the steady and unrepining duties of life may find it hard to believe in such atrocities. Unfortunately they know little of the working classes; only now and then, when some startling fact is brought before us, do we entertain even the suspicion that there is a society close to our own of which we are as completely ignorant as if it dwelt in another land, and spoke a different language, with which we never conversed, and in fact we never saw. Only in one way could this great danger, this great evil be counteracted. The religious sects must bury their differences. Let prudent spirit of conciliation enable the wise and the good, to offer to the people a beneficial education in the place of this abominable teacher.[5]

There are a number of concepts in this passage which we would not now link with educational discussions. In the twentieth century debates about education do not contain the open references to the threats of revolution; they do not warn so severely of the dangers of working people being educated by their surroundings; they fail to warn the state about the existence of communists always ready to subvert honest minds; yet it is not too difficult to show the links between such arguments and today's educational debates (in relation, for example, to educational priority areas).

Such reports at the time, though, were a direct attempt to alert the bourgeoisie of Great Britain to the problems that surrounded them all the time. At times of peace, such fears of revolt always seemed absurd, and at times of crisis their faith was in the militia, the special constables and the paraphernalia of repression. In warning the bourgeoisie in this way, *The Times* quite correctly indicated the changes necessary and that a national *state* education system would only result from the changed perception of this class.

The one group which was dedicated to the broadening of the horizons of the bourgeoisie to the problems of order caused by the working class was the inspectorate.[6] These individuals were employed to go and collect information on the working class and their habits. They were employed in a number of capacities: to act as a trouble-shooter after a strike or disturbance; to enquire into areas that were already seen as social problems—for example, the area of factory legislation; or to inspect the working of institutions supported by state money. All of these reports went to the central government over the period 1830–70; and to a very large extent they created the picture of working classes that the state had, since apart from these reports there was a large visual barrier between the state and the working class. These inspectors created the picture of a possibly turbulent working class, whose turbulence called for a system of education.

Now, how does this relate to the boys dolling off in Sunderland in the 1970s? How are their lives affected by the writings of a number of hard-working civil servants 120 years before? In looking at these reports we can see a particular *sort of education being proposed*: an education with specific aims in the direction of changing the lives and attitudes of the working class; an education which had as its hallmark a transference of a system of morality. In looking a great deal more closely at this mode of education I could see much more directly a number of traits that the boys of Sunderland in the 1970s found *the* disturbing thing about their educational experience. In this way I discovered it had become impossible to understand *why* boys dolled off without seeing what they were dolling off from; what they were dolling off from was explicable initially only in the historical terms of the creation of the education system that they were escaping from.

The nature of education destined for the working class

As *The Times* highlighted, it and the bourgeoisie were not simply in favour of 'learning' in general; rather they were interested in teaching only a specific form of education in a specific way. In looking at the inspectors' reports over thirty years we can see that there were a number of strands in this 'education' and that these were very directly linked to fears of insurrection.

1. The provision of bourgeois facts and theories to counter both 'revolutionary' facts and those facts that were derived from the material conditions of working-class existence at the time.
2. The provision of a bourgeois moral and religious code which, once it had been taught to the working class, would shape their behaviour.
3. The creation of a disciplined, punctual labour force.
4. The creation of a hierarchy of civilisation based upon education and refinement which the working class would respect and of which they would find themselves at the very bottom.

These arguments are put by others than the inspectorate; but it is this body which, against the background of accelerating growth in the political and industrial power of the working class, fed most into the state machine over this period.

1. Provision of useful bourgeois facts and theories

Throughout the 1830s private societies providing knowledge for the working classes were promoting what they referred to as 'useful' knowledge which was meant to enable the working classes to understand the world around them in a bourgeois way. These societies were aiming at filling what they conceived as a vacuum in the minds of working-class people; a vacuum which was seen as very dangerous if filled in a revolutionary way. Yet the trouble with such societies in terms of their efficiency was obvious: they were having difficulty in getting the facts into what they conceived as the vacuum in men's minds. Thus the provision of useful facts and theories could not simply be left to these societies; alternative sorts of agencies were needed. One of these agencies was the school.

Writing on the great miners' strike in Durham in 1844, Tremenheere reported that there was a lack of this kind of knowledge, so that when outside agitators came to the area trouble could be easily caused. This resulted in ' "Proprietors", and viewers, and agents who had been for years conspicuous as promoters of everything that could conduce to the welfare of the working population, finding themselves powerless against the misrepresentation of fact, and the erroneous arguments addressed to these men by their delegates and advisers'.[7] For people such as Tremenheere, then, it became important to explain how the working population of Durham could have risen up against their masters and, indeed, have seen their masters as people who were acting against their interests. Tremenheere saw the mine proprietors as benevolent men; the workers as honest men who were easily led astray. The strike he saw as caused by 'the excitability of their peculiar tone and temper of mind, and their liability to be led astray through their best feelings, in consequence of their present very limited state of intelligence'.[8] Obviously, then, the role of any counter-insurgency effort in Durham had to be aimed at countering this lack of intelligence in the shape of 'building schools, providing trained teachers, and opening schools at which payments are so moderate as to leave no excuse to parents for neglecting to send their children.'[9] However, crucially, as Tremenheere states earlier in his report, these children were in the main already being sent to school; so a desire for instruction was not sufficient, it had to be *correct* instruction — in other words, those facts, ideas and so on which were in accordance with the maintenance of the social order. 'The colliers tend, in general, to prefer sending their children to the old kind of day schools kept by men of their own class, though the charges are generally higher than at the new schools under trained masters. I saw many of these schools of the old kind. A few of the masters seemed to be fairly qualified to teach, in their own way, all they pretended to — reading, writing and arithmetic; but the majority of them are, as might be expected, men of very humble acquirements. The books they use are such as the parents choose to send. There can consequently be no regular courses of instruction in anything. The Bible or Testament is read but very little explanation is attempted. Each child is taught whatever catechism is brought with him.'10

One can see how horror-struck the inspector was at the 'anarchy of schoolrooms', where people brought the books that *they* wanted to read and learnt the religion and the morality that *they* brought with them. This was an 'education' (indeed, the quotation marks are those of Tremenheere himself) that failed to provide any real set of *structured* facts and theories for the working man. 'In all that related to a knowledge of the world around him, of the workings of society, of the many social and economic problems which must force themselves daily upon the attention of the working man, the mind of the growing youth was left to its own direction, and therefore liable to take up its facts and principles as chance might dictate. They are easily led into error, and persevere in it with the greater obstinacy because they want the knowledge to enable them to see where they are wrong.'11 In leaving the mind of the growing working class to find its own direction, it had, in Durham, come to the conclusion that 'their language was that the manufacturing power of the country was in their hands'.12

For Tremenheere, then, there was correct knowledge about society, and incorrect knowledge. He reported to the state and exhorted the coal owners of Durham that the way to stop the disturbances was to build schools to teach the correct facts and theories to the working man. Indeed, his reports are full of kind words for those wise employers who had built schools and employed trained teachers — this was seen as wise economy.

As the picture of these disputes grew over the century, more general statements could be made by these commentators. Continually, the specific lessons were being drawn to the attention of Parliament and the bourgeoisie. By the 1860s Kay-Shuttleworth was able to adopt a scornful tone in lecturing the opponents of a national system of education.

> We think it highly probable that persons and property will, in certain parts of the country, be exposed to violence as materially to effect the prosperity of our manufacture and commerce, and to diminish the stability of our political and social institutions. It is astonishing to us that the party calling themselves Conservatives should not lead the way in promoting the diffusion of that knowledge among the working classes which tends *beyond anything* else to promote the security of property and promote the maintenance of public order. [13]

The Royal Commission on Trade Unions in the 1860s lent even more support to Kay-Shuttleworth; for him, the ideas of trade union leaders confirmed the necessity of teaching bourgeois theories that would assist them in coming to terms with a class society.

> Parliament is again warned of how much the law needs the support of sound economic opinions and higher moral principles among certain classes of workmen and how influential a general system of public education might be in rearing a loyal, intelligent and Christian population. [14]

Illich[15] has recently coined the term 'the hidden curriculum' to stand for the ways in which schools change people's behaviour but which are not explicitly written into the curriculum. Between the 1840s and the 1870s this hidden curriculum was openly defined by educationists to whom it was obvious that schools had to 'teach educational skills, teach not only occupational skills, but also the nature of his domestic and social relations, his position in society, and the moral and religious duties appropriate to it'. [16] It was this curriculum which defined 'education' as providing in a certain sort of institution sets of ideas and theories which would lead working men to act in certain ways.

2. The substitution of bourgeois morality for working-class culture: the failure of the working-class family

Whenever the inspectors came across aspects of working-class culture they reacted in a very simplistic moral way. At all times, and seemingly about the most trivial things, the sports, the pastimes, the language and the lack of civility were commented upon. The inspectors particularly attacked provincial, regional dialect, and indistinct, to their ears, articulation. These expressions of disgust represented more than mere offences to bourgeois niceties, for they saw a clear political link between these expressions of working-class culture and language and the *apartness* of working-class life. This was described in similar way by Engels in 1844:

> In view of all this, it is not surprising that the working class had become a race wholly apart from the English bourgeoisie. The bourgeoisie has more in common with every other nation on earth than with the workers in whose midst it lives. The workers speak other dialects, have other thoughts and ideals, other customs and moral principles, a different religion and other politics than those of the bourgeoisie. Thus they are two radically disimilar nations as unlike as differences of race could make them.[17]

If this apartness, this difference, gained credence in terms of lifestyle it should represent a real alternative to bourgeois lifestyle. As such it represents a threat to the bourgeois world, and the tone of comment by the inspectors is more than the moral condemnation of *different* lifestyles.

The popular culture of the working class reflected not some simple moral maladroitness though, but their material conditions under urban capitalism. Working-class popular literature was condemned as 'obscene, exciting and irreligious works, letters and books [that] were complaining of the badness of the times'.[18] The public house was universally condemned for two reasons — not only 'the abuse of spirituous and fermented liquor', but also because they were recognised to be the local links of working-class economic and political organisations. They were places of resort 'for the pleasure of talking obscenity and scandal if not sedition amidst the fumes of gin and the roar of drunken associates'.[19] The links between obscenity and sedition, drink and politics, cemented the condemnation of working-class culture with the fear of revolutionary change. Thus the 'uplifting' of working-class culture was important in order to stabilise the political and social order.

In this line of reforming zeal, adolescence was always seen as the period of greatest moral peril, for it was during adolescence that the first signs of the combination of moral decadence and political instability showed itself. From all over the country inspectors reported the manifold misdoings of 'youths'. From the growing urban conglomerations the links between mob violence and moral depravity were confirmed in the state's vision of youth. One inspector diagnosed in the countryside a very close relationship between adolescent independence and rural incendiarism. Other important characteristics of youth were noted: their 'early financial independence, their tendency to take their values from bigger, rougher and more lawless boys, coupled with the general failure of parental control, and since the children did not honour and obey their parents, they showed no proper deference to their social superiors'. [20] Once more the direct link between immorality and political disobedience is clearly seen.

These state investigations widely identified the root cause of the problem as the failure of the working-class family; thus they centred their hope for the solution here too. Put simply, they believed that the elementary-school teacher should act as a substitute for the failing working-class parent. In the existing voluntary system of the middle of the nineteenth century, however,

The influence of the teacher of a day-school over the minds and habits of the children attending his school is too frequently counteracted by the evil example of parents or neighbours, and with the corrupting influence of companions with whom the children associate in the street and court in which they live. [21]

Thus the major aim of any national system of education was to equip the school *and the teacher* with a means of combating these influences, and to carry out his role fully as a bourgeois substitute. This placing of the teacher *in loco parentis*, then, is a distinct attempt to ensure that the child gets a correct moral training in the face of incorrect parental working-class training.

Johnson sums this up in a brilliant article:

For Fletcher [an inspector] the school must be essentially a foreign implantation within a commonly barbarised population. It should rest not in the satisfaction of an indigenous demand but upon aggressive movements on the part of the better elements of society. The essential character of the whole educational project is caught in Fletcher's description of the school as 'a little artificial world of virtuous exertion'.[22]

This parental substitution by the middle-class teacher has been one of the hallmarks of the educational attack upon working-class culture. The results of this substitution have become one of the major concerns of educationalists since. But it is the *results* only, rather than the historical process as a whole, that have interested the educationalists, so that today educationists are greatly interested in what they see as a failure on the part of the working-class family to assist the child at school. But in these historical terms it is possible to see that this is in some sense inevitable, since the educational system was designed not simply to be different from the working-class family; rather it was designed to *attack* the basis of that family, and substitute a different authority for it. This relationship is crucial to our discussion in the next chapter about behaviour in school.

3. The creation of a disciplined labour force

The nineteenth century had seen a number of crucial developments in the system of production, as well as in the way of life of the mass of the people. The factory system of production was essential to the making of profit by industrialists, and this system needed a much tighter form of discipline from its labour force.

Thus issues such as punctuality became matters of intense importance. But this discipline did not flow naturally from the living conditions of working people. Most of the new factory operatives had been uprooted from the rural backgrounds and were now living in the extreme disorder of the new urban capitalism. Such ideological and material conditions were conducive to anything but the discipline needed by the factory owners; thus the creation and formation of that discipline proved one of the major and continuing problems.

The first need of society is order. If order is to be produced in men and women, what kind of preparation is it that leaves the children as wild as young ostriches in the desert? When, for the first 10 or 12 years of life, there has been no discipline either in life or body, when cleanliness has been unknown, when no law of God or man has been considered sacred but direct physical force — is it to be expected that they will quietly and industriously settle down in mills, workshops, warehouses or at any trade in the orderly routine of any family, to work continuously by day, morning and evening, from Monday until Saturday? The expectation is absurd. Continuous labour and sober thoughts are alike impossible to them.[23]

It was necessary to ensure that the years of 'the young ostriches' were spent in ordered pursuits.

In some of the mills where schools have been established and attendance regularly enforced the mill-owners have assured me that great improvements in the conduct and habits of the children had been evident and that the difficulties were not so great as they apprehended![24]

and

I am assured that the younger classes, in every case where their education is based upon any sound and regular system, are deriving much benefit from it, and that the training consequent upon such order and regularity, is securing a greater degree of subordination than was expected.[25]

Thus the discipline taught in schools rests not only on the simple philosophy of discipline being 'good for you' in an abstract way, but is also closely tied to a particular *form* of discipline. This would solve only the problem of a *particular class* of people.

4.　The creation of a national hierarchy based upon education

The nineteenth century saw a continuing struggle for power between three separate classes — the industrial bourgeoisie, the working class and the aristocracy. This power struggle took many forms — in economic terms, in terms of naked street power on occasions, in Parliamentary terms and in terms of ideologies. The period saw continuing attempts by the bourgeoisie to create a unified ideology.[26] The need for this ideology became paramount whenever there was any weakening of the bourgeois position in the other forms of struggle. One of the necessities of this ideology was to replace the feudal hierarchy which had seen the aristocrat firmly in charge; it was now necessary to create an ideology which would ensure the continued ascendency of the bourgeoisie.

With the passing of the 1867 Reform Act and the enfranchisement of the urban working class, the calls for an education system became even more strident. Robert Lowe, an educational administrator who had opposed the extension of the franchise, felt that once the working class had been given the vote, education was a necessary concomitant. Lowe lauched a series of speeches and pamphlets based upon the belief that 'It was absolutely necessary to compel our future masters to learn their letters'.[27] He urged not only the formation of schools, the levying of a compulsory rate for their maintenance and compulsory attendance, but also the complete overhaul of upper-class education on the same grounds. This latter education system should teach the upper classes sufficiently well to 'know the things that working men know, only know them infinitely better in their principles and their details'. This knowledge would allow them to 'assert their superiority over the workers, a superiority assured by greater intelligence and greater civilisation', so that they can 'conquer back by means of a wider and more enlightened cultivation some of the influence which they have lost by political change'.[28]

Thus Lowe states with crystal clarity that political reasons must dictate educational change; he is equally clear about the class system that it is to serve. It is essential that the working classes be educated so that they might defer to a higher cultivation when they meet it, and the upper classes ought to be educated in a very different manner in order that they may 'exhibit to the lower classes that higher education to which, if it were shown to them, they would bow down and defer'.[29]

Thus the education system was to be created in such a way that the working classes would subordinate themselves to a hierarchy of 'civilisation' with their own agreement.

Some readers may well be convinced by now of the nature of the education system in the nineteenth century. Yet they may well feel that things have changed now; in the 1970s education is concerned with individual development, and cares for each person within its control within the terms of their own culture. But the discussions outlined above are not of a purely academic interest. The quotations come from people who were taking part in something more than a simple debate about the nature of education. These individuals were taking part in a struggle to define what 'education' was and what it wasn't. By taking part in this political struggle they succeeded in setting the parameters of the educational debate over the next 100 years. To provide an example of the rigidity with which these parameters were set, the reader need only ask a number of questions about education that were considered relevant before state education. Should all age groups be taught together from the ages of three to 73? Should parents be allowed to pick the books which their children learn from? Should the sorts of knowledge and the organisation of that knowledge be decided by parents? Next time you go to a school, try asking the headteacher some of these questions and see his reactions. Does he feel that these are relevant 'educational' questions nowadays? Of course not.

The way in which education is considered has been well within the guidelines drawn up over the period outlined in this chapter. There have remained a number of obvious traits, though, in the educational debate which can identify these continuations.

Education is still about changing individuals; it is about challenging some of the 'bad cultural traits' of sections of the population. Nowadays such discussion takes place in terms of the failure of the family — a failure highlighted in the nineteenth century. If we look at Butler's presentation of his Education Act in 1944 we can see some of this ideology at work, despite his apparent protestations:

> Here I want to make it clear that it is no part of the Government's policy to supplant the home. I should like indignantly to repudiate any suggestion that that is our policy. But unfortunately, the experience of evacuation and other war experiences have shown that many homes need helping. [30]

Such a view of the relationship between school and parents has been echoed many times before and many times since 1944. The homes that need helping would not be those of cabinet ministers, but those that were betrayed by the evacuation from large cities during the war. The working-class homes of the urban poor.

Looking at the Newsom Report of the 1960s we see once more only a change in the nature of language, but no significant change in the conception of education.

> The picture which these headmasters have so movingly drawn for us makes it clear that the social challenge they have to meet comes

from the whole neighbourhood in which they work and not from a
handful of difficult families.[31]

Again,

> Most schools clearly have the welfare of their pupils very much at
> heart. The problem of serious indiscipline is relatively small, and
> most intractable in the areas where the social forces outside are
> working against the school.[32]

The relationship between area and school in these quotations still
emerges as one of challenge, of attempted change. The success of this
challenge can be seen from a later paragraph in the Newsom Report
where magistrates are chided for not giving the parents of truants
bigger fines:

> It is essential that magistrates should appreciate that in this
> exercise of their function they are part of the educational system
> and have a responsibility to support it.[33]

Now if we accept the whole nature of the educational system and of
the state that it is a part of, then we can accept its attempts to improve
on the nature of the society around the schools. If, however, we
question the nature of that education and see that some aspects of it
that are NOT an attempt to improve the pupils' lives, then we must
deeply question and analyse the nature of the state–education
relationship. If we do not, then the children still do; they experience it
as imposition, as some form of attack. Are we to deny them the right
to know what is happening to them between 9 a.m. and 4 p.m.?

It seems clear from the historical account that schools are relating
to the children *despite* the major material experiences of their
background; that there is a powerful strand within state education in
this country which sees its role as transforming the culture that is
created by those material experiences; that the moves to child-
centred education are changes which are tactical rather than
strategic, in that they take the children's immediate world and relate
ideas to it, rather than looking at the underlying relationships that
create that world. Therefore there are strands within the education
system that are divorced from the material relationships of the
children and are in actuality trying to change the children's culture

and ideas. It is hardly surprising under these circumstances that school is experienced as imposition.

Returning to the boys in Sunderland, then, they highlight in their answers to questions about truancy the overall experience of education as an imposition. This imposition is not the *whole* explanation of education; it does not mean that all teachers get up every morning and aim to change working-class children into paragons of bourgeois virtue. It does, however, form an element of the whole nature of education which must be understood in this overall way.

3
Why do kids muck about in class?

In looking at truancy I have been trying to answer a question about activities taking up a small percentage of school life. However, being IN the classroom and being educated by the teacher are two very different things. In any analysis of conflict it becomes important to understand the amount of 'passive resistance' and 'non-cooperation' that goes on. In the classrooms of the British education system this is called, variously, 'mucking about in class' and 'not paying attention'. Far from being a minority activity, this constitutes a majority activity, for much of the time, for the boys. Therefore truancy must be seen as an extreme action; 'dolling off' as less extreme; 'mucking about' as a major activity and 'not paying attention' as endemic. The way in which such 'misbehaviour' is viewed in the contemporary period is also important.

Classroom misbehaviour has become of increasing significance not least for its perceived effect upon the success of the school as an academic institution. Recently it has sprung into importance with what appears to be a growing amount of violence against teachers, special schools being set up for 'troublesome pupils'.

There has been a great deal of political interpretation of the causes of this violence. Right-wing educationalists blame the overall collapse of authority wrought by 'left-wing permissive teachers'.

Reasons for the violence and general misbehaviour have been spelt out in many different ways. The political correspondent of *The Times* has worried himself about it recently in terms of the increasing influence of socialists in the field of education and the failure of conservatives to fight the battle of ideas in our schools. Thus we have seen a direct linking of politics and education. There are a welter of alternative explanations, many of which are generated by different sorts of sociological explanations over the past thirty years.

The 1950s saw a large amount of research into the relationship between home and school; how the working-class home did not provide the correct background for the working-class pupil to get on at school. The remedy for this was to change the working-class home a bit and (later in the 1960s) to change the school a bit too so that it became more welcoming for the pupil from that class background. My own initial view of classroom misbehaviour was only slightly more sophisticated than this.

Colin Lacey and David Hargreaves[1] had created in the 1960s a view of the relationship between working-class home and secondary schools which intruded another variable into this explanation. They both were interested in the ways in which a counter-culture developed, and how this counter-culture developed around working-class boys. I went into my Sunderland research interested in why working-class boys should be the ones that represented the counter-culture so consistently. The answers that I expected were in terms of their rejection of the school values and the creation of an internal culture based upon that rejection. Thus similarly to my initial argument about truancy, I expected to find the boys striving for school values; unable to achieve these values; and turning them on their head to create their counter-culture. This argument linked with that about working-class homes detracting from their children's educational opportunities. It was their *cultural background* which I took as the factor which stopped the kids from attaining school values. Try as they may it was not possible for them to come to grips with the sort of thing that the schools were asking of them.

In my research, then, I was looking for the initial acceptance and later rejection of school values. In the classroom the school values confront the pupils all the time and try to shape their behaviour and attitudes; therefore it was in the classroom interaction that I was looking for the signs of this process of rejection and creation of new values. I was looking for this explanation in the boys' attitudes to school in general and their teachers in particular.

Almost immediately after coming into contact with the boys I could see the errors in this explanation. There seemed to be no real acceptance of school values by a lot of the boys *at any time*. In fact, the whole emphasis on 'values' as a guide for action seemed to be wrong. The boys' actions were not created by such consistent things as 'values'; the crucial factor to explain classroom interaction seemed to be much more to do with the power differential between teachers and pupils.

Most importantly, this power relationship was played out between groups of people who were in the institution for different reasons. As we saw in the last chapter boys were only really at school because they had to be. Given that, it became important to see how the boys coped with being in an institution which they could not really see the point of.

The power relationships in secondary schools have recently become an issue of great political importance. Starting within the field of educational politics there was an attack by the right upon what they saw as an increasing liberalisation in our education system. This attack was highlighted by the 'Black Paper' on education.[2] At the same time many individuals on the right who had previously been interested mainly in politics also became concerned about the long-term political effect on the structure of our society of years of liberalisation in the nation's secondary schools. The two leading figures of the rightists' counter-attack are Rhodes Boyson, who has now entered Parliament from being headmaster of Highbury Grove; and Ronald Butt, the political correspondent of *The Times*, who now takes up column inches detailing the failure of 'our schools'. This has put classroom misbehaviour right into the centre of the political map, where it has not been for over a hundred years. Interestingly, Rhodes Boyson and Butt take the part of such political educationists as Robert Lowe and such educational politicians as Kay-Shuttleworth. Correct behaviour in the classroom teaches correct behaviour in society at large; incorrect behaviour in the classroom leads to anarchy in society at large. Their fears are the fears of the founding fathers of education – we must look at classroom misbehaviour in this light.

In looking at the way the boys in Sunderland actually coped with school, it became obvious that there was not total unanimity of opposition to the school or to the school's values. Some boys did express attitudes, ideas and actions about their education which could be described as positive. However, it is important to see precisely how these boys experienced their education, in order to see more precisely the way in which the education system meets their needs.

In trying to find out all the boys' attitudes to school, I baulked at the question 'Do you like school?' as a totally inadequate way of talking about their experience. The abstractness of this sort of question has, I think, been the downfall of much sociological research. It represents the distance between the experience being talked about and the more abstract concepts of the sociologist. It is necessary, even in something as inadequate as a set of written questions, to try and recreate in the person's mind a real, experienced situation rather than a pure abstract feeling. In an attempt to overcome this I asked them a question about an experience which had always encapsulated, for me at any rate, my attitude to school: 'At the start of a new term are you glad to be coming back to school?', followed by 'Why do you feel this way?' Also 'Will you be glad when you have finally left school?', followed by 'Why do you feel this way?'

Initially the answers to the first question came as a surprise in that 48 boys were glad to be returning with only 44 not glad. This apparently betrayed a great joy at the start of a school term which did not seem to be reflected in their attitudes and behaviour in the field of truancy. However, any analysis of their answers to why they felt this way showed a different set of ideas about the end of the holidays. I coded these within five sets of answers:

See my friends at school	7
Get bored during the holidays	29
Pro-school	10
Anti-school	31
Pro-holidays	13
No answer	3

Thus of the majority of boys who wanted to come back to school only ten felt any pro-school feelings ('I am glad to get back because when I leave school I hope to have a good set of qualifications for a job' – *Richard*; 'I am glad to come back to school because I like the lessons' – *Peter*). Most of those looking forward to the commencement of term talked in terms of the boredom of holidays ('I am glad to be coming back to school because I am bored with the holidays' – *Adam*) and the attraction of friends at the school ('Yes, well, sometimes it's boring and you have friends there' – *Derek*).

In the interviews I followed this up by asking the same question, and the boys had a better chance to express themselves. One boy explained the rewarding nature of school very clearly.

Question   In the list of questions I asked you, you said that you were glad to be coming back to school at the start of a new term. Why do you feel this way?
Robert   Well, you learn more things and it gives you a better chance for a job, and if your holidays could be, like, instead of six weeks in

the summer and two weeks at Christmas it would be better, like, if it were four weeks at Christmas and four weeks in the summer as then you still get the same amount of study in.

Question So you think that the important thing about school is the amount of study that you can get in?

Robert Especially for the jobs nowadays as even in the shipyards you need C. S. E.

Question Why do you think that some boys get better qualifications than others?

Robert Some boys get better qualifications as they understand the work more easy than other people, such as in maths. I might be able to get a few right but I can't understand it. It's just the way different teachers explain it.

Question So it's a combination of being able to understand it and the way the teachers explain it. I mean, why is it that you can't get the idea of maths; is it because of you or the teachers?

Robert Well, last year when I was in 3H2 the teacher was Mr Haroldson; he wasn't going mathematical all the way if you couldn't understand anything; he used to change it to English or something like that. But now with 4Al with Mr Willerby he sticks mainly in mathematical terms as 4Al is just like the group that he had last year except for about four people.

Robert appears to find the educational experience rewarding within the terms of the system itself. The process of working hard for better qualifications is more fully explained in Chapter 4, but it is important to mention here that certain boys experienced school this way and not in totally conflictual terms. There was no boy who expressed total support for the school on all the ideas and actions. They did tend to like to work in class rather than talk; they thought that the teachers actively helped them when they had problems. They also were condemnatory of their peers when they took part in certain activities; truancy was actively 'bad', a boy who was cheeky with teacher was 'wrong to do it'; overall this group felt that many of their pupils interfered with the smooth running of the school.

It becomes important, therefore, in attempting to understand the totality of working-class experience of the state education system to try and understand what these boys get out of their educational experience. For example, does Robert back up the original theory outlined at the beginning of the chapter? Does he in fact fit into Hargreaves's academic subculture?[3] Does he agree with the values of the school and act in accordance with these values? I would say that this explanation does not help us to understand this group of boys. There is no evidence at all of these boys seeing education as useful for its own sake; as seeing learning and knowledge as important; or, indeed, of their learning a set of moral rules by which they will live their lives. Instead, those that found the experience rewarding, found it rewarding in a *specific* way; they saw that through education they could get better jobs. In the chapter on careers I talk about the important causal chain of events that the school tries to get across to the boys. If you behave yourself, you are more likely to work hard; if you work hard, you are more likely to do well at school; if you do well at school, you will get good qualifications and a good reference; if you get a good reference, you will get a good job; if you get a good job, then you are likely to get lots of money. For this group of boys that causal chain is their reward from their school experience. They talk all the time of the links between behaviour and the material rewards at work when they leave. Thus it is possible to see that, for these boys at any rate, the school does provide them with a rationale which they find acceptable, and that they shape their behaviour accordingly. Importantly, though, this co-operation with the school remains at *this* level; at no stage is there evidence from these boys that they have internalised all the *values* of the school.

Indeed, they stop short of the sort of co-operation with the education system which is expected by teachers and which would make the system work a lot smoother. Only seven boys said that they would tell the teacher in order to stop one of their friends getting beaten up by a group of boys. So even to save a friend of theirs from being 'done over' they would not call in the authority of the school. In any understanding of acting on the school values this must count as a very small amount. Similarly in completing the sentence 'In class I like to . . .', they completed it in an ambivalent way; 'In class I like to talk and do my work' – *Peter*; something that the teacher may well feel is incorrect.

Of these boys I think we can say that they work along with the school as long as they can directly make the link with what *they* see as the rewards of their behaviour. If they feel that that link is not there in the case of certain sorts of behaviour then they are not likely to co-operate with the school.

For most of the boys that I got to know and talked to, though, there was no real continuing form of co-operation with the school; the boys all seemed to fit into Hargreaves' model of the delinquescent subculture.[4] It is important to see precisely *why* the boys thought this way. To do this I asked a great deal about specific experiences of school.

Teachers as 'big-heads'

When I first started the research I was surprised at the consistency with which the boys used the phrase 'big-heads' to describe the teachers. I immediately thought that the use of this word represented a school-bound fashion (that is, all teachers in Municipal School are called by the label 'big-head' as part of the tradition of the school rather than with any explicit meaning). Consequently, I specifically asked boys in the interviews about the phrase and the way that they experienced the teacher.

The phrase 'big-head' does imply a different sort of relationship from other forms of derogatory-relationship words. Thus it is possible for the boys to say 'I think teachers are . . . smelly', which conveys the derogatory idea but without the connotations of 'big-head'. The answers when the boys were asked to complete the sentence 'I think teachers are . . .' split this way:

Derogatory personal	38	(Big-heads; bastards; fucking crap; smelly and ugly)
Derogatory professional	21	(Bad teachers; too strict; useless as teachers)
All right	16	(Not too bad; all right)
Good	13	(Good; good teachers)
No answer	5	

The distinction between the first two groups is based upon the language used about the teacher rather than any substantive distinction; I will go on to show that I think when the boys criticise Mr Brown for being a 'fucking bastard' they are criticising him for being a *teacher*, even though they may not specifically use a derogatory *professional* remark. Eighteen boys intimated that they thought teachers were 'show-offs' and 'big-heads'. The remaining derogatory personal remarks were startling in their viciousness. Throughout, I was surprised at the little swearing that went on in most of the answers that the boys gave. Most of the swearing that went on was about their opinions of teachers. ('Teachers are fucking crap' – *Ian*; 'Bastards' –*Ivan*; 'Fucking mad' – *Charlie P.*; 'A load of shit' — *Fred S.*; 'Smelly and ugly' —*Dick B.*; 'Pigs' —*Albert.*) Now, as with truancy, we are all inured by years of reading comics to the fact that boys dislike teachers. It is one of the 'stands-to-reason' pieces of knowledge about our society. However, it is important when confronted with answers like this to try and understand why such viciousness is expressed, rather than simply accepting it with an indulgent wink about young people.

Much criticism, though, was in a more sober language and was about the professional competence of the teachers. These varied from talking about specific grievances ('Not fair because they treat girls different from boys' —*Mike N.*) to the little more generalised complaint ('Very misunderstanding; not friendly' — *Bill*; 'Too strict' — *Dave*; 'Too soft' — *Bruce*) to the totally generalised ('Terrible teachers' — *Steve*). Those boys who reserved their judgements were either grudging ('All right for teachers' — *Douglas*), more specific and extreme ('Some are all right, some are bastards' — *Wyn*), or even tautological ('Quite good because they are not always bad' — *David*). Those who liked the teachers tended to be specific ('Mainly good and nicely treating teachers' — *John*; 'Very understanding' — *Eric*).

The important question of discipline and sanctions is dealt with elsewhere. What is also important here is the experience of the teacher that lay behind the boys' experience of discipline, rules and so on. Thus two statements were included for the boys to check off:

Teachers don't really care	Strongly agree	17
what happens to me;	Agree	45
they are just doing a job	Disagree	19
	Strongly disagree	9
	No answer	3
Teachers don't understand the boys	Strongly agree	28
	Agree	39
	Disagree	15
	Strongly disagree	7
	No answer	4

This creates the impression that two-thirds of the boys experience the teacher as someone who is quite distant from them and only brought into contact with them by their job. Thus *the interactions of the classroom must be seen as financially compulsory for the teacher and legally compulsory for the boys.*

However, it is important to remember that the boys do not simply experience the teachers as a group of people who are different from themselves and don't really understand them; rather the teachers are seen as a group who are different from the boys and *have some power over their lives* and who believe that they are right in trying to change their behaviour. These two aspects of the teacher – difference and power over the boys – provide us with the clue to understanding the phrase 'big-head' and to coming to terms with the viciousness expressed by the boys. This comes out even more clearly in the interviews:

Question Do you think teachers understand boys?
William I don't think that they understand. They are just a long way away.
Question What do you mean?
William I . . . dunno . . . just not like us and they push us around.
Question Some boys said that they thought that teachers were 'big-heads'.
William Yes, because they crack us. I got a crack today in metalwork.
Question What was that for?
William Mr Hills when he comes past anybody he just cracks them.
Question Any reason?
William No, he just cracks them. Sometimes he uses a piece of wood. Don't need no reason.

Question Do you think teachers understand boys?
Jimmy Some of them don't, they just hit you for anything. As I said, some teachers you like, have a bit of fun with, but some others don't understand you if you're bored or anything like that.
Question Some boys thought teachers were 'big-heads'. What do you think?
Jimmy Some of them are, like Mr Withers, and they pick on you for anything. Even if you walk around the streets they tell you to get on the pavements or something. If you're talking or carrying on in the town some teachers tell you to shut up and that. It's nothing to do with them. Last Saturday I was told to shut up by Mr Blackford in town. It had nothing to do with him, that's just 'cos I was carrying on.

In these two interviews the idea of distance between the teacher and the boys is coupled with the *power* that the teacher has in his position as a teacher to impose those differences upon the boys. The power to try and challenge the boys' behaviour is specifically vested in him by the education system, created within the ideologies outlined in the last chapter. There is no perception of the teacher – pupil interaction as being a joint 'coming together' of minds. Rather, there is a great distance between Them and Us; despite this, They push Us around. One boy took the trouble to explain the whole process to me step by step.

Question   Do you think teachers understand boys?
Edward   Well, like the way the boys act, the teachers don't understand 'cos some of the teachers are old, and in any case they are different from us, and we're young and have got our own ways. They don't know what it's like to be young and live on this estate.
Question   In the questionnaire you said that you thought that teachers were 'big-heads'.
Edward   Well, some are because they think, Ah, they're a teacher and they think that they can rule you in school and tell you what to do and where to go and all that.
Question   Do many of the boys not like this?
Edward   Aye, hordes of them don't, because the teachers are always picking on them and that.
Question   Are you going to stay on at all?
Edward   No, I'm leaving this summer.

The process that the boys see happening to human beings who become 'teachers' is that they think 'Ah, I am a teacher, I can rule you'. This relationship and view of the teacher is different from the one seen in the *Beano*. Obviously it is a banality simply to say that boys dislike teachers; but here we can see that the boys dislike and criticise Mr Bloggs, not because he individually is 'smelly', but because he fulfils the role of teacher, he acts as a teacher and believes he can rule you. The boys say then that the *distance* between pupils precludes any meaningful relationship, because it is a distance which takes place alongside a specific power relationship.

This raises the question of the legitimacy of the teacher. This sort of topic is much discussed in the sociology of education but the process of legitimacy is one that I found had no recognition by the boys. Teachers pushed the boys around and the boys didn't like it; they tried to rule the boys in class and outside in the streets, and in both places it wasn't liked. The boys saw the teachers as doing a job which specifically included pushing them around. The 'authority' of the teacher was important for the boys in terms of the control of their behaviour. This control was seen in terms of the amount of power that the teachers could wield. One boy even went further than this: he defined those people that failed to push you around as not real teachers.

Question   You said that you thought that some teachers were 'big-heads'. Why did you say that?
John S.   The way that they go on, like. Like Mr Jones, like he talks on and then he gets you out the front and puts his walking stick around you, just goes, ah, like that [imitates putting crook of stick around your head]. He thinks he can just push you around. Some of them are 'big-heads' but some of them are all right. Only they're not like teachers, they don't push you around.

So, those individuals that don't push the boys around aren't seen as real teachers. This seems to represent a very shrewd appraisal of what a 'teacher' is in their experience of 'schools'. The role of teacher is within the education system set up and outlined in the last chapter: *inextricably* linked with the idea that someone pushes you around.

Within this relationship, then, dislike for teachers expressed with a great vehemence and anger is *not* simply a childish reaction to authority but represents an experience of the situation of school similar to that encountered by the people who created the education system. Both sets of people defined this in terms of changing boys' ways of life – one group define it favourably, whilst the boys define in unfavourably. In this light the phrase 'teacher is a shit' cannot be dismissed as a simple reaction of a 'boys-will-be-boys' nature; it must be seen as a rejection of the right of someone from a great social distance to try and change the boys' lifestyle.

If we compare the boys' words with the hypothesis outlined at the beginning of the chapter we see very little support for any of the ideas expressed there so far. Instead of the boys ever trying to attain the school values, we see little reference to the values at all, whether those of academic or delinquent *school* variety. Instead, at this stage of the research I started to realise that education for these boys was not concerning itself so much with delinquent or academic *values* at all; instead, the educational experience was defined by power, and an attempt to make sense of the boys' words in terms of values at all produces results only by imposing a set of ideas.

Understanding classroom interaction

In order to understand the ways in which the boys deal with the day-to-day activity of going to school, we must see them as involved in a relationship with the power of the school and the teacher. In my questionnaire I asked a number of questions about classroom action. These were not simple descriptions of their action, but represented some attitudes about certain forms of classroom action. In the interviews I followed this up with a wider system of questions.

Thus this sentence-completion question is about the ways in which boys immediately feel about their activity in class:

In class I like to . . .	Muck about	54
	Work and play	12
	Work	23
	No answer	4

This shows immediately at least a sharp differentiation between what the boys feel their best activity is in classroom, and what the teacher feels it is. The activities that they did enjoy at school were very varied; a number simply said 'talk to my friends', or 'talk'. Here we see a set of activities which are at one and the same time natural and forbidden in the classroom situation. To talk to one's friends is not something which social scientists generally feel is problematic and worth explaining; yet in the context of the classroom such activity does need explanation. It is explicable for these boys, though, *only* in terms of the need for silence to enable the teacher to teach and control the class; within this rationale it is obvious that teaching is disrupted and it must be forbidden. Also, given that the boys' talking in this situation is likely to lead to them being hit, the fact that they like to do it does need some interpretation. It reflects, I think, the boys' relationship with the variety of sanctions that the school uses to enforce its rules, since there is talking and talking; to carry out a simple and open conversation might lead to immediate punishment, so techniques of talking to one's friends must be introduced to ensure that sanctions are avoided. The continuation of talking to friends when it is forbidden betrays the importance and meaning of this activity in relation to the wider social relationships of the school. To talk to one's friends is a continuation of activity that is considered quite normal on the street. It is simply continued here in a context that does not allow it.

So talking in class represents a set of contradictory meanings; it is a continuation of ordinary activity, yet is abnormal because the institution of the school does change the *mode* of communication. In other words, it is a naïve activity carried out in such a way that it is *transformed* by the power of sanctions. My impressions of talking with the boys is that most of the motivation for talking in class represents a simple continuation of outside activity.

Question What's carrying on in class?
Ivan Well, it's just talking. As we would outside, I suppose. Carrying on . . . just talking, shouting in classrooms.

Much of the other preferred classroom activity is similar to talking in that it represents a normal activity made abnormal by the situation of the classroom. The most obvious is eating. It at first appeared odd to me that any number of boys would reply that in class they liked to eat, since I would not link the action of eating necessarily with any classroom activity. Yet it merely represents a continuance of their outside activity. They do *know* that it is a forbidden activity in classrooms. Once more, though, knowing it is forbidden is NOT to say that they see it as *wrong*. Forbidden means that the rule has to be enforced, and the question is one of *surveillance* for the teacher; and *tactics* for the boys in continuing this normal activity. Once more the activity is affected by the power of ban but not by the idea of wrongness.

There are sets of classroom activities which are much more concerned with the actual situation of school. Those boys that said that they looked forward to returning to school because they enjoyed mucking the teacher about are showing a different attitude to the activities of school. The teacher and the school are a much greater part of their behaviour; it is very much affected by the classroom situation and the rules. Similarly there are some aspects of 'talking' that are aimed at the teacher, so it becomes important to see two different sets of actions that are against the rules of the school: on the one hand, activities that are simply carried on from the outside and are incidentally banned by the school; and, on the other, activities which are directly attacking school regulations. Thus rather than seeing all rule-breaking behaviour as similarly caused it is important to see some as merely defensive behaviour and some as attacking.

This difference can be outlined by the phrase 'carrying on in class'. In the interview I played the ignorant southerner and asked them what such a phrase meant. It became clear that in general sense there were two sorts of activities in classrooms — that initiated by teachers, and 'carrying on'.

Question   Lots of boys said that they 'carried on in class'. I've not heard this phrase before. What does it mean?
Dick   It means just not bothering about what the teacher says; if one boy gets told to stop doing it, then someone over the other side of the room starts. When he looks over to them you start doing it again.

This represents the major single point that I learnt from the research: that it is impossible to extricate the behaviour of the individual from the power situation. 'Carrying on' represents *at one and the same time* taking no notice of the teacher, being aware of the teacher's power, and doing what the teacher doesn't want you to do. The only link between these three is that the boy is asserting his right, in the given power situation of the classroom, to take part in whatever action he feels like. That action is not dominated by values of a pro- or anti-school nature; instead it is about the power situation perceived and experienced in that school. Given that for the boys the teachers are 'big-heads', and they try to rule you, the boys are presented with a problem of initiating their own action. To start using the analogy of a guerrilla struggle, 'carrying on in class' represents the ability of the boys to continue their normal way of life despite the occupying army of the teachers and the power of the school, *as well as* their ability to attack the teachers on the boys' own terms:

Question   Lots of boys . . . carrying on. What does it mean?
Bert   Taking the mickey out of teachers. Taking it to them, carrying on.

Tactics and strategy for defence and attack in the classroom are developed over time. There are some teachers that the boys can attack all the time and can feel confident of attacking. It is an interesting glimpse of the counter-insurgency strategy tactics used by teachers to ward off the attacks:

Question   Lots of boys . . . carrying on in class. What do they mean by this?
Ian   Running about in classrooms, underneath chairs and things like that.

Question   What do teachers do about it?
Ian   They'll come in and probably pick on the softest boy out of the whole class, sort of thing. I could tell you an instance: the other week, there were some boys in class tossing chairs about. Teacher walked in and he asked one of the toughest boys what was happening and he says, 'I won't tell you'. So he went off automatically and asked a softer boy.

Here the teacher is betraying the tactic of control that 'automatically' puts pressure upon the weakest of his opposition in an attempt to get information. Equally the boy who says 'I won't tell you' is basing his defence upon his knowledge of the teacher's weakness.

In this analysis, even when the boys are simply carrying on with a normal activity from outside, it represents an attack upon the authority of the school. It is important in analysing school behaviour to remember that at all times the instigation of the interaction is in the hands of the teacher and the school, NOT with the pupil. In other words, the institution is there to change the boys, which is the reason for their compulsory attendance. Consequently any refusal by them to change their behaviour within the classroom is a *direct reversal* of the attempted rationale of the institution.

Question   Lots of boys . . . carrying on. What does it mean?
Tony   Well, it means that we do what we do outside class. Talk, shout, eat, muck about. Just what we always do.
Question   What do the teachers do?
Tony   They don't like it. But what can they do? They can't rule you, can they?

So the onus is left entirely upon the powerful forces in the school to enforce the rationale of the place: 'they can't rule you, can they'; no, but they can have a good try.

Question   Lots of boys . . . carrying on. What does it mean?
Jimmy   Yes, you get put on report for that. If you get bored in a lesson and that, an' you have a bit of a carry on, flicking paper around, you get wronged for that and put on report and you get caned.

Therefore, they CAN'T rule you but they can *try and stop you.* Once more the dominance of punishment and sanctions becomes clear: they can stop you from doing something by use of power and surveillance, which is again the only method of guerrilla control.

Question   Lots of boys . . . carrying on. What does it mean?
Wyn   Just have a good laugh. Have a fight with the girls, you know.
Question   What does the teacher do about this?
Wyn   Teacher doesn't know; we always do it when the teacher has turned his back to the board or something.

How are these tactics evolved? Obviously there is no handbook written by a schoolboy Guevara. Rather, it evolves over a period of time. Where there are no 'documents' and 'briefing sessions' it becomes an appallingly difficult job actually to decipher the ways in which tactics are evolved.

To try and get some of this information, I asked the boys to imagine that a new boy started in their class. What advice would he give him about his school? Given the existence of a naïve boy in your class you immediately tell him those things without which school is an impossible situation to fathom.

Question   Imagine a boy joined your class. What advice would you give him?
James   I'd tell him about the teachers that were soft and how we carry on with them. And I'd say, watch out for that teacher as he is hard. Just things that he had to know and let him find out the rest in his own time.
Question   There are 'things he *has* to know' –like?
Bert   I'd just tell him to watch for some of the teachers. Like Mr Jones, who takes fits; just tell him not to say anything wrong to him or he will jump on you. He hit a lad down the stairs.
Derek M.   Just tell him to watch out for some of the teachers, and tell him what he can get away with and what he can't.
Charlie   Just tell him not to let teachers push him around. Those he can carry on with as he wants, and those he has to watch.

Some of the teachers therefore have to be watched, others you can carry on with as you like. Importantly, you needn't be pushed around, because the boys have a store of knowledge about the weaknesses and strengths of the teachers, which allows them to combat them despite their superior power. Even given the 'obvious-ness' of such ideas, teachers and sociologists of education still expect boys to be primarily interested in the *content* of their education. Yet this is not the case, they do not say 'Maths is interesting but geography dull' to the new boy in the class; rather they specify which teachers you can carry on with as normal and which you have to watch. So, boys do experience school as an institution primarily designed to try and change them; in much the same way as the early educational experts saw school as an attempt to try and change working-class boys.

Punishment and sanctions. What the school does when the campaign to win the hearts and minds of the working class fails . . .

Given the attitudes of the boys that I have outlined so far, it is becoming obvious that the only possible way to make sense of their words and actions is in terms of the *power* of the school rather than its values. This is a crucially different way of viewing the boys' behaviour, for it puts a premium on the ways in which the boys actually cope with these sanctions. In the school's terms, it is trying to change the minds of the boys to get them to behave in a more civilised way; if it is not possible to get them to regulate themselves then the role of outside sanctions becomes much more important. To get at the boys' perceptions of what happens in this area at school, I asked them what happens if they do something wrong.

When I do something	Hits me	32
wrong my teacher . . .	Takes a fit	19
	Employs rational discipline	25
	Helps me to put it right	8
	No answer	9

In answering this question only eight out of 93 boys saw their teacher as primarily assisting them to learn their lessons. The others saw a person who, in a variety of different ways, was there to enforce any broken rules with a variety of sanctions. It is the boys' perceptions of these sanctions that are under review here. It must be remembered that these represent, not a simple addendum to an institution of learning, but the part of the experience of school which assumes primary importance. It is history and geography, maths and English that are experienced as periphery; the experience focuses on rules, sanctions and discipline. The teachers are seen as enforcing their discipline in three main ways: by violence; by losing of temper; or by the application of a rational set of rules. The boys' attitudes to the use of violence are very interesting and slightly surprising to someone outside their situation. Given the boys' lifestyles and their overall participation in fights and so on, it is surprising that they were so indignant at the use of physical force against them by the teachers. Yet it was the *conditions* under which the violence was committed on them that angered them rather than the violence itself. Simply put, they felt it was not right to be hit under circumstances which forbade the counter-punch to the teacher; not being allowed to hit back made the interchange unfair. Overall I would say that there was no evidence of an overarching set of moral values about violence; instead these working-class kids had a set of more pragmatic ideas on the subject. The sanctions experienced from the teachers were different. The physical violence stretched from the old faithfuls ('Canes me' – *Pete*) to the more to hand ('Cracks me' – *Fred S.*) and the more exotic ('Chucks rulers at me' – *Paul*; 'Hits me with his walking stick' – *James*). The losing of temper was expressed by a variety of phrases ('Takes a bloody fit' – *Dick*; 'Tries to get funny' – *Michael*; 'Takes a rage' – *Edward*) and simply ('Goes mad' – *Rupert*). The rational mode of discipline is one that stretches from the mild ('Lectures me' – *John*) through a whole series of sanctions ('Gives us extra homework' – *Tom*; 'Keeps me in detention' – *Stanley*; 'Takes me to the head of house' – *Peter*) until finally ('Will send me to the Headmaster' – *Tim*). Whilst all three of these are experienced differently, it is possible for us to lose sight of the vital point that these are *sanctions* created to attempt to coerce people into behaving differently, by using different sorts of violence.

Given that over one-third of the boys experienced the teacher having recourse to violence when they did something wrong, they were asked how often people *were* hit in their class.

Are boys hit	Every class	12
very often	Every day	39
in your class?	Every week	32
How often?	No answer	10
What sort of	Carrying on in class (cheeky, talking, carrying on)	63
things are they	Something special in class (swearing, homework)	8
hit for?	Something passive in class (not paying attention)	8
	Something active outside of class (smoking, dolling off)	7
	Bad behaviour	5
	No answer	2

The second question greatly underlines some of the points made above about the relationship between teachers and boys. Violence on the part of the teacher is carried out mainly for behaviour in the classroom which is a continuation of normal behaviour outside of that classroom. It is THIS which threatens the teacher most. Violence is used to try to enforce a certain view of the sorts of activities which *should take place in the classroom* – that is, it is a place where there is silence, where boys pay attention to the teacher, where boys are not cheeking the teacher. It also represents a perception of the use of violence in creating the necessary conditions under which the teachers can teach discipline. It is interesting what violence is NOT used for. It isn't used to instil geography, history, maths or science; rather it is used to instil quiet and respect. The intensity of the boys' experience of education can be shown by their opinions about teachers that use violence.

A teacher that hits you is . . .	A big-head and a bully (a bastard, a twat, a puff)	62
	Descriptive (not a good teacher)	13
	Right (doing his job, doing the right thing)	10
	No answer	8

Again the viciousness of the school interaction is highlighted by the disgust that the boys feel about teachers that use violence. On several occasions it is referred to as unfair – not that they are appealing to non-violence but because the activity of physical violence on the part of the teacher allows the boy no right of reply. If the teacher were to allow physical violence to flow both ways in the classroom then I think that there would be a different attitude – indeed, given the feelings of these boys there would be very few teachers who would continue to use violence in the classroom! It was important to try and gauge the boys' perceptions of the rationale behind the teachers' punishment of boys.

Why do you think teachers punish boys?	To make them obey rules	22
	So they don't do it again	35
	They are bastards and they lose their temper	23
	No answer	15

These answers are, crucially, located in the boys' perceptions of the teachers' rationale. In the interview I asked the boys whether they thought that punishing boys to teach them right from wrong worked or not. It is very important to note that *everybody* interviewed said that they thought punishment did not teach either them or other boys right from wrong. This was a *unanimous* opinion of all the boys: punishments did not teach rules. Indeed, most of the boys laughed scornfully at the idea when asked about it as if the idea struck them as familiar but absurd. The complete universality of this argument must undermine one of the most popular models of control in the education system.

There were three main sets of answers to the question of why punishment.

Discipline

Question　Why do you think that teachers punish boys?
Ivan　It's like this. They are trying to make us see what they think is right from wrong. First they just tell us, and then they punish us to teach us it, since we don't listen much. They say it's just to teach us right from wrong.
Question　Does it work?
Ivan　No, it doesn't teach us anything.

So the teachers first try and simply tell them what is right and wrong from their point of view and then try and reinforce that with a rather crude Pavlovian stimulus response model of behaviour. But the boys say that it doesn't work. It doesn't work simply to tell them; it doesn't work to hit them into it, either.

Question　Why do you think that teachers punish boys?
Ian　I suppose it's just a sort of discipline but I don't think that it does any good. I mean, if you look in the school book you see that the same boys get the cane all the time. It mustn't be working.
Question　Do you think the teachers think it works?
Ian　Yes, it must satisfy them. But it doesn't seem to satisfy the boys that get into trouble (laughs).

In this way the simple empirical investigation of looking in the book proves that the teachers' claim about discipline and punishment is invalidated.

Punishment as retribution and deterrent

Question Why do you think that teachers punish boys?
Dick I couldn't say really. Some of them punish boys to get you back for things that they say that you shouldn't be doing, dolling off and that, but if they are gonna punish you for dolling off their own lesson you'll get punished as well by the head of house and Mr Smith as well!
Question Some boys thought that teachers punished boys to stop them from doing it again. Do you think that it works?
Dick No, well, it doesn't work with me. The first time I dolled off, there was about five of us and two of them got caught. Well, last Wednesday afternoon one of the lads that got caught was dolling off with me again.

Therefore the idea that punishment as a retribution for past wrong acts as a deterrent is not valid for these boys. As stressed in the last chapter on truancy, the boys will obey power and sanctions only as far as they feel that there is the power to enforce them. In other words if they feel that they can do it without getting caught they will do it without regard to past experiences of punishment for the same offence.

Punishment as maliciousness, as lost temper

Question Why do you think teachers punish boys?
Jimmy I don't know. Because they don't like them. I think that some teachers just pick on me and my mates in the class for nothing.
Question Some boys said that they thought that teachers punished boys to stop them from doing things again. Do you think that this works?
Jimmy I don't know about that. Sometimes I am just sitting at the back of the class and I get wronged for talking, *and* it was a boring lesson. In careers when the teacher is talking he goes on for hours and we are bored and we like to talk. If you're bored I reckon it's fair enough to talk and no amount of getting wronged will stop me.

Therefore, given the capriciousness of a teacher who picks on you for talking when he has been boring you into talking, the boys feel that it cannot possibly teach them not to talk.

Control in the classroom

How, then, are we able to understand the way in which boys are controlled in school? There are four different ways in which the school and the education system try to control the behaviour of these boys.

1.   The first model is the one that most educationalists would dearly like to see work. I have styled this 'the attempts to win the hearts and minds of the working class'. This model attempts to teach the boys, by a variety of techniques, the appropriate norms and middle-class values upon which rules of behaviour should be based.

Thus rather than simply teaching the boy the rule of respecting the teacher, it is better to get him to believe that all figures of authority, who wear collars and ties, are worthy of respect – rather than teaching him to be quiet in class, you teach him that it is rude to speak unless spoken too; rather than teaching him that he must get to school by 9 o'clock, you teach him that he must always regulate his life punctually. In other words this represents a direct attempt to create certain forms of action (and to destroy certain other forms) by providing the boys with a coherent set of values on which always to base their action.

In this model the school is meant to be a civilising agency within the community as a whole; it was intended to make the action of the working-class boys both *inside and outside the school* those that conform to different values. This was an ambitious task by the state and the middle class; yet a task which is still pursued and believed in by sections of the state and the ruling class. The measure of the 'failure' of the schools to carry out this function for the state can be seen in the fact that the school itself, the agency that was used to win the hearts and minds of the working class, cannot even ensure the use of these values by the boys *within its own walls.* Thus if the teachers had succeeded in changing the boys' attitudes, values and actions to their own, not only would the boys' actions on the street, in the youth club, at the football ground be the very model of bourgeois civilisation, but it would also be so at school. Instead the picture that I get of the actions and attitudes of these boys towards anything that remotely seems to be 'bourgeois civilisation' is at least one of total ignorance and, in an angry minority, one of disgust.

This failure of the education system has ramifications for the remainder of this book; it has failed to get across a conception of a career and ambition; it has failed to get across an idea of useful, structured leisure activity; it will inevitably fail, given the structure of an education system that mirrors a structure of a society. The social policy effects of this inevitable failure will be outlined in the concluding chapters. However, it is important to underline here some of the reasons why this failure is *inevitable*. Returning to the nineteenth century:

> It is evidently unnecessary for us to talk about enlightening the operatives, and instructing the mass of the population. We may go to sleep as far as that is concerned. They will not wait for our instructions. They will instruct themselves. They are self-sufficient and until far better instructors appear than most of those who manifested themselves, we cannot blame them for being so. Prophets are raised up to them 'of their own brethren' and why should they listen to the voice of the stranger. Let them teach one another. [5]

The educational relationship outlined within this quote runs counter to the policy of education created by our society and enshrined within its schools. However, as far as my research shows, the setting up of the education system has *not* stopped the education of the boys continuing outside their schools. But the continuation of the boys' activities in learning from their experience at home and with their mates has meant that their lives and their understanding of their lives is *based upon a different way of seeing the world* from that of the school. Given the existence of this way of seeing the world it is impossible for the school to impose its values and ideas, as the *techniques, form and content* of school are experienced then as an attempt to rule. This attempt to rule, given the learnt existence of working-class culture, is at least passively, and at times most actively, resisted. It is the nature of this imposition and resistance which sets the tone for all school classroom activity between working-class boys and an education system geared to changing those boys.

For the moment, though, we are talking about the techniques of control attempted inside the school. Recognising that it is not possible simply to transfer the values and sentiments of the middle class to the working class, the teachers are still confronted with a problem of order *inside* the school.

2. The second model of control is based upon the attempt by the

school to teach *rules* themselves to the boys. It is hoped that these rules will be understood as they are intended – that is, as guides to action. Thus this model of control still hinges on the belief that boys will change their action and behaviour according to 'rules' or 'ideas'. However, as one boy said ('First they just tell us, and then they punish us to teach us it, since we don't listen much' – *Ivan*) the words and ideas that the teachers try to communicate are not in fact communicated, because the listening and understanding necessary for rules to be communicated do not take place. Educationalists and sociologists alike make the mistake of assuming a simplistic relationship between agreeing with general rules as 'right' and allowing these totally to govern action. In another field of state control, many trade unionists, when asked by opinion pollsters whether they thought unofficial strikes should be made illegal, agreed. However, when this generalised agreement is put to the test in terms of their own experience of struggling in the industrial world, it does not affect their actions in a one-for-one way. Similarly, even those kids who agreed with certain school rules did not let them greatly affect their actions. In a way this failure is, like the first model, inevitable. If someone *teaches* a set of rules which are intended to change people's actions, then those rules come from outside the culture and experience of those people. Since in the first place ideas and rules spring from the experiences of people (one learns about fire and hands this way) the experiences which lead the teacher to recommend that punctuality is a good thing are not the experiences of the boys. So a rule created from one set of experiences cannot simply be imposed and learnt for another set of experiences. Boys will say that they think the rule is a good thing, but since it is created at such distance from their behaviour they do so automatically. So teaching rules *per se* does not control behaviour.

3.   This is why the third method of control is realistically created, within the school. This links the teaching of rules with one simple and important addition – the punishment of the offender after each infraction of the rule. This model rests on the aversion therapy model worked out by B. F. Skinner[6] which claims that if you punish a boy severely after he breaks a rule he will link the breaking of the rule with the punishment in his memory and automatically check his action in the future. Once more, though in a different way, this model is based upon the control over action by the mind governed by rules. In this case it is the *sanctions* rather than the particular *rules* which are the

factor which stops rule-breaking behaviour. In the chapter on truancy, this came across in the experience of having to go to school. The sanctions had been raised to such a level that the boys obeyed the rule of going to school because they were afraid of the consequences of infraction. However, even though we can see the power of this model over the boys' behaviour, when compared to the other two, it does not control their behaviour in anything like a total sense. For, even though this model does rest upon the power of the teacher to enforce sanctions the crucial difficulty for the teacher is catching the boy breaking the rule, or enforcing the sanction. Given the concrete situation of the school, the boy finds that he can easily break the 'broken rule–automatic sanction' link. This is broken by the tactical outmanoeuvring of a small powerful body, the teachers. Thus they evade detection for 'dolling off' and for all broken rules and, if caught, try to plead innocence. Given the success of these out-manoeuvrings, the boys know that they can break the rules with impunity *if they don't get caught.* So, rule-enforcement hinges on the difficulty of ensuring that the boys get caught.

There was, though, a minority of boys who were controlled by this model; they were cowed by the *possibility* of getting caught and punished; and it was this possibility which stopped them from acting in such a way as they would be punished. These boys, then, were prepared to be controlled by the teachers. This is not to say that they learnt the school values, or that they learnt the ways in which rules can govern behaviour; rather they were simply afraid.

4.   However, for most of the boys a fourth method of control was necessary to keep order within the school. This was constant surveillance. Building on the failure of the first three methods of control, this simply says that a rule can be enforced only in the presence of the person enforcing it. It stresses the fear of punishment, not in a general sense or in a sense linked to rules, but rather linked to a fear of getting caught. This puts a great deal of pressure upon methods of surveillance and is time-consuming for those in control. Rule-enforcement and rule-breaking become a totally creative process linked to the different sorts of power involved in the situation. The power and imagination of the controlled are pitted against the power and imagination of those controlling. It is this method that the boys accepted as the method that controlled them and controlled their friends' actions.

This has tremendous implications for the teaching profession and for the interaction of all our schools, which I will deal with in a later chapter. Suffice it to say here that such a technique of control can ONLY be implemented by having teachers constantly on their toes and, in this way, exhausting themselves.

The success of such a method as the fourth MUST be seen against the failure of the other three and the reasons for their failure, which stems from the policy of attempting to impose an education system on the working class which is specifically designed to change, to civilise, their behaviour. Given such an education system, the conflict that ensues is written into every school. It does not come down to the internalisation or otherwise of values; rather it hinges on the power of the members of one group to create a situation where they try and impose those values in order to change actions. Given that it is the power of one group to commence the interaction which is important, my research shows that it is equally the power of working-class boys to refuse that imposition which creates the parameters of classroom interaction. The only alternative to this conflict is for the education system to win completely and for the boys' attitudes and behaviour to change. However, such a variety is becoming less and less likely bearing in mind the evidence of conflict within our schools. Indeed, it would appear that, with the failure of the first and second models of control, our schools will increasingly resemble a battlefield, and a battlefield where the boys will more and more be on the winning side.

In trying to come to terms with these different methods of control within the school it is easy to see why the one most constantly used, that of constant surveillance, led me to the seemingly incongruous analogy of guerrilla warfare for behaviour in the school. That there was conflict became obvious; that this conflict was not *resolved* by the use of the power of the teacher and the law was equally obvious. The question became, 'What is the source of the power which challenges the teacher?' Youthful exuberance would have wilted early on in the battle; the schoolboy naughtiness of the *Beano* would not have lasted the first use of headmasterly power. It is explicable only in terms of the complete refusal to allow oneself to be taken over by the ideology of the school, and the use of superior numbers to run the teachers into the ground. These different sorts of power began to coincide very clearly with the different sorts of power exercised in a guerilla struggle: a heavy amount of state power is overwhelming in itself but it has to be made to have its effect; the response to this comes from a larger number of individuals who occasionally act together, but mainly act passively against this power, attempting to reject its effect. The guerrilla forces act within their own ideology of resistance, one which is usually deemed as irrational by the state powers; they use heartlands from which to attack the state power, heartlands which are mainly inaccessible to the agents of the state. For a long time in all these struggles, unless there is intrusion from outside, a position of stalemate can become normal, with each side winning the occasional victory, imposing the occasional set of casualties. Teachers and pupils in secondary schools at the moment will recognise this analogy as a day-to-day reality.

Why do boys choose dead-end jobs?

Most people reading this book, if they have to think about getting a job, have been schooled to think in terms of 'careers'. In thinking in these terms we automatically start thinking about 'choice'. Nowadays, many radical people reject the idea of career, of a lifetime's service to a job, and many of the sociology students whom I teach specifically refuse to enter jobs that may lead to this role. However, even these individuals see their opportunities (and the rejection of them) in terms of their own choice. Given this almost total ideology amongst the most middle-class section of society, it is nearly inevitable that 15-year-old boys will be understood in these ways. Thus we automatically apply the sorts of thinking that we use about our own life to that of these 15-year-old working-class lads. Sociology too has attempted to slot their 'choices' into our categories: one boy 'chooses' to be a plumber rather than an electrician; another 'chooses' the mines rather than the merchant marine. It is believed to operate in the same way as university graduates 'choose' teaching or becoming a finance capitalist or publisher.

In talking to these boys I very quickly found out that this system of thinking does not coincide with theirs. In the last year at school the boys' attentions are increasingly drawn towards their future. Visits by careers advisers become more frequent, teachers spend more time with the boys talking about their future jobs. Out of this activity, each boy is meant to create a clear vision of his future 'career'. This represents an important moment in the boy's life, since his choice shows the way in which he thinks about the non-school world. Sociologists have spent some time trying to make sense of this time of boys' lives both for reasons intrinsic to their choice of work and for reasons affecting their wider life.

Thus a whole set of studies has been directed towards discovering why certain boys choose certain jobs, looking for the way in which they are directed towards these particular forms of living. There have also been a lot of studies of how boys view the whole structure of job opportunities. Lastly a great deal of attention has been focused on the ways in which the boys feel about the differential access to the better rewards offered by society for different types of jobs; these perceptions have then been linked with certain forms of delinquent and deviant behaviour.

All of these studies helped to create my interest in the boys' choices of career. Would it be true that certain sorts of boys choose certain types of employment? Would the more intelligent boys talk about their future.work in terms of the satisfaction of the job rather than the cash nexus? Would some boys see the world as being divided on class lines, seeing this as a major cause and justification for smashing up telephone boxes? It was these questions that I wanted answered by my study. Like many of the other questions, I discovered very quickly that they were not the sort of questions that had any relevance to the ways in which the boys lived their lives.

Why choose certain jobs?

In the studies on how boys see their future careers there were four major forms of job choice – inner-directed, other-directed, tradition-directed and a residual category called uncertain choice. The inner-directed choice represents a boy who chooses his future work on the basis of some personal interest in or involvement with certain hobbies. An obvious example is a boy who has always enjoyed work with wood and felt able to express himself through amateur carpentry; he would be likely to become a carpenter. An other-directed lad will choose because he has been advised to go into a certain form of employment, by a parent, a careers master or an elder brother, for example; he will choose to become a carpenter because the careers master suggests it as a good job. Tradition-directed covers those boys who feel that their choice springs from their background – that is, because their father has been a carpenter or because their whole street have been carpenters. The last category of uncertain choice is admitted by one of the writers, Maizels,[1] to be much more likely to cover those boys from manual-worker backgrounds who have been uncertain as to their abilities and interests and apprehensive as to whether they would like or be suitable for certain kinds of employment.

It was these categories that I expected to be able to validate by looking at careers.

How do the boys see the whole job structure?

It would seem to be commonsense that if a boy chooses a certain form of job he will have some idea about the whole way in which people get different jobs. This has been styled the 'opportunity structure' and the way in which the boys see it has been thought to affect their whole set of actions. Thus if the boys see that certain people are getting a better chance of success in society, they are more likely to feel hard done by and angry. It is important not only to find out how they perceive the different jobs but also to see the ways in which they see people getting access to these jobs. There have been a variety of studies on this topic, most of them originating in the United States. Boys have been asked not only 'What job are you choosing to do?' but also 'What job would you like to do?', 'What job would you choose to do of all the possible ones?' and lastly 'How do different people get these better jobs?' There have been a variety of answers to these questions but a form of sociological orthodoxy emerges which helped me to draw up my ideas to put to the boys of Sunderland. Firstly, it would appear that boys tend actually to *expect* to get jobs which represent very closely the jobs that they will get. In other words, their expectations tie in pretty closely with their probable careers. Secondly, though, their perceptions of the opportunity structure lead them to believe that there are indeed much better jobs than these that they *aspire* to in their fantasies. Thus a gap develops between their expectations and their aspirations. This gap tends to lead to certain forms of frustration. Thirdly, though, they tend to see that everyone has an equal chance of getting at all these jobs and that their failure to get to the better jobs therefore reflects their own personal failure. These perennial contradictions stem from failures of society to link up their *structural* and cultural parts: 'We suggest that many lower-class male adolescents experience desperation born of the certainty that their position in the economic structure is relatively fixed and immutable – a desperation made all the more poignant by their exposure to a cultural ideology in which failure to orient oneself upward is regarded as a moral defect and failure to become mobile proof of it.'[2] Thus in Sunderland I'd expected to find a number of boys who had experienced great personal failure by not availing themselves of *what they saw* as an egalitarian structure of education. This frustration has been seen as one of the major causes of delinquent behaviour in the young, and therefore become very important to try and gauge.

How do the boys see their future choice of work?

All the information taken from these boys was taken in the year before most of them left school. For some of them only a few days were left before they embarked upon their career. It is at this stage that they are under the most pressure from both inside and outside school to think constructively about their future work. Given the fact that three-quarters of the boys in this study were really looking forward to leaving school, one would assume that their minds were very firmly directed to the future. This would be especially so since 62 per cent gave reasons for wanting to leave that could be classified as pro-work. However, the single most important finding that struck me in terms of the boys' ideas about their future work was that thinking about their future jobs was of very little importance to them. With certain exceptions, their answers in both the questionnaires and the interviews showed no overall picture of occupational aspiration – or of thinking very much at all about their future. There was almost no mention at all of the process of work itself as an important reason for leaving school; rather, most of those who mentioned work as a reason specified the *rewards* of work, and this in a very specific way ('To get some money in my pocket' – *Peter*; 'I will be bringing money in and helping my family' – *Arthur*; 'I can go out to work, get money and enjoy myself' – *Dave*; 'When you are working you have your own money instead of pocket money from your parents' – *Harold*). Therefore, the concrete results of getting a job when you leave school are those that can be imagined at the time – namely, more money in your pocket to spend in the way in which you spend it now. Indeed the word pocket, when linked with money, represents a much more concrete experience than the idea of a wage packet. It is not money in the abstract that they want, but more of the sort of money that they experience now. The process can be summed up in two more answers ('I will be glad to leave school to earn a man's wage that will result in more pocket money for me' – *Duncan*; 'Well, I would like money so that I can get some more clothes and that, and so that I can go places with my friends' – *Paul D.*)

What is interesting is that here I was specifically interested in the ways in which boys thought about school and not their future jobs; when asking them about that I framed the question very much in terms of the sort of ideas outlined by previous social scientists. Therefore I framed the question: 'People do different jobs for different reasons; which of the following do you think is the MOST important reason for any job you do?' In this question I was making a number of presuppositions which I now feel were incorrect. I presupposed that people did jobs for various *reasons* and that they selected their employment on this basis. Similarly, ideas like 'reason' and 'choice' do not necessarily play any part in the actual experience of getting a job for working-class youth. Thus if we look at the boys a few years later it is very unlikely that these particular boys will ever ask the question 'Why do people work?' They are more likely to make it a lot more personal and more brutal: 'Why the hell am I doing this job?' If my question which contained the ideas of reason and choice had tapped any consistent strain of thought in the boys, then one would expect that to be reflected in the set of other questions asked about their future work and their perceptions of the opportunity structure. 'What work do you expect to be doing?' 'Do you think that you will be doing this job all your life?' 'If you will change it, what to and why?' 'People do different jobs for different reasons; which is the MOST important? (interesting, well-paid, friendly workmates, promotion)' 'If you could choose any job, what would you be?' 'Sometimes we all dream about being things we know we shall never be; what do you dream about?'

All of these questions do in fact represent different areas of the reality of 'thinking about jobs' for the 14-year-old. The prospect of leaving school is not as enlivened by getting out to work as by the prospect of an increase in pocket money; in these boys' minds work does not contain anything intrinsically attractive. None, for instance, specified that they wanted to leave school so that they could go out to work by itself. Yet 29 per cent specified that the most important REASON for CHOOSING a job must be that it is interesting. If we were to expect a thoroughly consistent attitude to their prospects of future work, then we would see this as a contradiction. Yet, as we shall see, there are a whole series of contradictions that run through all of the boys' answers, contradictions which are surprising only if one assumes that there is a concrete set of occupational choices and aspirations for these boys. One thing is clear from this set of answers: there is no clear, hard-and-fast REASONED CHOICE for these boys. As I got to know them it became very clear that the whole concept of a career had a minimal relevance to the way in which these boys lived their lives.

The relationship that emerged between these boys and their future employment was a very different one.

What do you expect	Professional	8
to be doing when	Skilled	24
you leave school?	Unskilled	29
	Services	17
	No answer	15

It is not easy to compare this data with other studies since my interest was self-consciously concerned with working-class boys and their 'careers'. There are, however, a much larger number of boys entering the services (other studies have suggested only 2 per cent) and a smaller number expecting to enter skilled manual work. Both of these characteristics are explicable in terms of the local working-class community culture. The recruitment for the Army and Navy represents an important tradition in an area racked by prolonged structural unemployment. This is reinforced by two factors. Firstly, the boys expected that it would be difficult for them to get a job (48 per cent thought this) and in this atmosphere going into the Army is one of the safer bets for single men. Secondly, when I moved to the north-east, I was immediately struck by the amount of recruiting done by the services every July and August. All the big towns in the area have large numbers of tanks, field guns, and so forth in strategic places at this time of the year. Thus the 'choice' of the Army or Navy by these lads is affected by these structural and cultural factors that are interplaying on one another. The rise in unemployment reduces the 'choice'; the Army advertises more in areas of unemployment; parents and relatives not only talk of their good times in the Army but also argue that it teaches you a trade; the Army pushes its apprenticeship role, etc.

The lads that did expect to go into the services were generally the exception to the diffuse aspiration model I have outlined. Most of them knew why they expected to join the services, and in the interviews showed a great number of links with the services. The most extreme case was Robert:

Question Why do you want to join the Army?
Robert Well, it's just that I've been going down the Army cadets since I was two; and even me mum used to carry me down when I was one and it's just that I've liked the Army ever since, and what with

taking cookery at school I just fancy the Catering Corps. It's also where you get the best qualifications.

Question   What sort of things do you like about the Army?

Robert   Well, it's the action and that.

Question   Even in catering?

Robert   Even in catering there is action.

Question   Do you want to get promoted?

Robert   I'm getting a stripe already.

   This lad gave a thoroughgoing, consistent set of answers that represented why he wanted to go in the Army. Promotion was his *reason* for selecting a job; he chose to be a soldier out of all his visions of the job market. In my experience this was limited to only those boys heading for the services.

   If we look, even with these boys, at the categories set up in the studies mentioned earlier about the boys' choices, then we can see their failure. Is this boy, tradition-, inner- or other-directed? Looking at him we can see the absurdity in real life of any of these splits. If a boy likes playing with guns and at soldiers and wants to base his career on it, it is likely that he will have a father and relatives who reinforce the interest and who will reinforce this choice of a job. Thus we have the seemingly inevitable collapse of the inner- and the tradition-directed. Similarly, it is more than likely that any careers master will at least know a little about his boys' interests and backgrounds; given this, he is more than likely to base his other-directing advice on this background knowledge. Overall it becomes very difficult to pick out a simple causal analysis of why boys end up in certain jobs. The picture is one within the general cultural limitations of boys seeing their future work as part of a chance configuration of family, careers and traditionally known job opportunities in the area.

   This 'chance' is structured by the boys' immediate environment. This comes out very clearly in two examples:

Arthur   At first I wanted a job where I was an electrician but my dad says that there is not much money there and there is a man that said that he would get us a job with his firm (he has his own firm) as a plumber, and me mum says that every week I have to pop round and see him.

Question   Are you interested in the money or the job itself?

Arthur   Well, both really. I'd always wanted to be an electrician but me mum said that there was more money in plumbing and I could serve time as an apprentice.

Question Have you got a job?
Brian I've been down to see about going to the pit but I don't think that I will. I want to get away from school but I want a decent job. I'm not bothered how hard the work is. I just want the money.
Question When I came to the north-east I was surprised at the number of boys joining the Army; have you ever thought of joining the Army?
Brian About three weeks ago in careers I was reading about the Royal Navy and it said that you didn't have to have qualifications to get in, so I took an address down. I told me dad and he said 'It's no good asking your mother, she'll not like the idea. You could ask to join the Army but she won't let you go in, so it's no good asking her'.

Here we have two cases of boys who, it must be remembered, are at most five months away from leaving school, switching their expected jobs after only one additional piece of information. In both cases we can see the effect of mum upon the process; this is not to say that mum is the determining agent in selection, just that mum has got the strength of an expert in these matters – she is not to be questioned. In the first case we have a lad who has wanted to be an electrician all his life (someone who we would therefore expect to have a deeper commitment than most to his job expectation) being prepared to change it because his mum says that there is more money in plumbing (which does not of course necessarily reflect the true position in the average wages for the two jobs).

When I turned to expectations of job mobility it may appear at first sight that an overall *commitment* to a certain sort of job *does* in fact emerge. 48 per cent answered yes to the question 'Do you think that you will be doing this job all your life?' (42 per cent answered no, 10 per cent didn't know). If we were to analyse this response in terms of a middle-class model of careers, it would represent a high degree of commitment. However, there are other alternatives which make more sense of these kids' expectations. The next question asked 'If you think you will change your job, why will you change it and what to?' The answers were classified as follows:

Why change?		What change to?	
Fed up/bored	17	Same level	20
More money	11	Promotion	8
Better job	4	Change to 'star' job*	5
Miscellaneous	12	Don't know what to	11
Don't know why and won't change	48	Won't change	48

* A 'star' job is one linked with extreme success, often in rock and roll or football.

When confronted with a lifetime at the same job – and these jobs it must be remembered are not the sort of work where you are given an increment at the end of each year, or where there is a career structure to work one's way up – only four out of 92 boys said that they would move in order to get a better job. 20 per cent specified that they expected to change because of the boring nature of their work. This was said with varying degrees of confidence ('I'll get sick of the same thing' – motor mechanic, *Brian M.*; 'Because you get sick of it' – P. E. teacher, *Roland*; 'Because I'll get bored' – engineering, *Bert*; 'Because it will drag on and on, the same old thing' – factory workshop, *Steven*; 'Because I will get sick of it' – change from Navy to baker, *Chris*; 'Because I might get sick of one job, the first one that I came to' – merchant navy to vanboy, *Pat*). For nearly all of these boys, then, the expectations of changing their jobs does not represent occupational mobility in the sense of rising up the social-status scale, nor does it represent any expectation of increase in wealth or change in lifestyle.

For most of them there are expectations of a lifetime in the same job, and those who do shift will be doing it for an increase in wages or a touch of variety. Again, we get a picture of no expectations of job satisfaction or career trajectory in any way. Instead we see what has been described as the instrumental working-class attitude to work, or alternatively the expectation of alienated labour. Neither of these two paradigms represents the working classes' actual experience of the labour market since the Industrial Revolution.

If we look at the expectations of what their jobs will change to, we get a similar picture: not one of a career ladder, but one of horizontal change. The change from shopfitter to sheet-metal worker, or postman to bus driver shows once more the lack of any conception of bourgeois career patterns; rather, it shows a simple recognition of a boredom-induced change.

**The boys' job expectations in relation to the way they see the job
structure**

In asking the boys 'If you could choose any job what would you
choose to be?' I was attempting to gauge some form of frustration
from their expectations. I coded their answers in the following way:

Same as expected job	27
Same level as expected job	11
Promotion from expected job	23
A 'star' job	15
Services	2
No answer	15

An immediate interpretation of this data supports the idea that
there is a large gap between the expected jobs and the jobs that boys
would really want if given a free choice. Thus, possibly there is a
group of boys 40 per cent of whom have a disjunction between their
wishes and their expectations. Yet if we look closer at this group there
are many contradictions *within* it. This group of 38 boys split 47 per
cent–53 per cent as to whether they expected to be doing their job all
their lives; nor do they justify their expectations or their aspirations in
any consistent way. If we look in more detail at the individual
answers, an even more fragmented picture emerges. Of those who
chose a job entailing promotion two groups emerge: those who chose
promotion within their expected job (agricultural college to race-
horse trainer – *Derek*; bakery to cook – *Dave*; Army to General –
Tony; engineering to higher grade of engineering officer – *Frank*);
and those who chose a job that entailed a change of industry (motor
mechanic to a potato business – *Brian M.*; plumber to naval
architect – *Arthur*). The 'star' choice split fairly evenly into brain
surgeon, footballer and a miscellaneous rag-bag. These three groups
obviously each have very different meanings attached to their
answers, and it is these meanings that represent important data.

For those in the group which chose promotion in their own job,
there was no real frustration since they saw their first job as part of a
ladder to their 'dream' job. For those in the second group (a group of
nine) there does seem to be a real gap between the job that they would
really like and the job which they expect. It is this group that we
would expect to be involved in delinquent activity, if the original
frustration hypothesis is correct. Yet I could find no evidence that this

group was in any way more frustrated or generally annoyed than the rest of the boys. Equally, those in this group at no stage and in no area engaged in any more delinquent activity than their less ambitious friends. They represented, as far as deviant activity both inside and outside the school is concerned, a typical group.

Those that aspired to a 'star' job rather than one requiring promotion call for a different set of culturally specific explanations. The number of people mentioning brain surgeon as their dream job is surprising, especially so when one considers that no other medical job was ever mentioned. An explanation springs from the boys' own culture. In the *Daily Mirror* there is a strip cartoon about schoolchildren called 'The Perishers'. Featured in this cartoon is a character called Marlon who, despite constant attempts by his friends, parents and teachers to persuade him to the contrary, keeps saying that he wants to be a brain surgeon when he grows up. Marlon is portrayed as being very stupid and this occupational choice is seen as confirming his stupidity. Thus the mention of brain surgeon must be seen in this cultural milieu – it is essentially a joke. The choice of footballer represents a much longer-standing cultural goal of working-class youth.

To conclude this part I would like to reiterate some of the points made earlier. Firstly, it is of paramount importance NOT to transfer the model of a career from one's own experience to that of the working-class youth. It is only possible to make sense of their job expectations if viewed in the light of their own experience and their own culture. If this is not done the sociologist will inevitably create a picture of working-class boys as deviating from a careerist model that would really apply to himself. The researcher will be constantly amazed at the mundane level of choices of these working-class kids, since he is working on his own perceptions of the labour market within his own perceptions of choice. These perceptions are class-bound ones; it is necessary to rearrange them completely to make sense of these boys' ideas about future work.

Secondly, there seems little validity in creating a classification system of the reasons boys have for choosing employment when we have already called into question the very structure of 'reasoned choice of jobs'. When I came into close contact with the real world of job choices it was clear that there were severe limitations to such classifications in adding to our understanding. This is because a classification of 'reasons' can only work when those reasons are a concrete part of the process that actually leads up to the expected employment. In the case of the boys that I got to know, with the exception of some of those bound for the Services, there were no real reasons to be classified. The answer to the question 'Why does Arthur end up in this job?' is part of a *process* and as such it must be the whole process that we try to understand. Once more it was the boys who had taught me that simply to ask a boy for a reason, classify that reason, and then believe that you have classified social reality, does great violence to the way in which the boys experience the process of 'getting into jobs.'

The process of getting a job was not one in which these boys had reasons. You HAD to get a job, just as you HAD to eat. There were no reasons for this inevitability. Any 'reasons' or 'causes' articulated by the boys must be viewed in these lights; they must be seen as clues to help us understand their reality, rather than as that reality itself. If we see them otherwise, the reality that we create is at a very great distance from the reality experienced by these boys.

The boys' perception of 'opportunity structures'

One of the major difficulties that confronted me was to come to grips with the ways in which the boys understood the whole job structure. Did they in fact see the world as one of equality of opportunity? Or did such an ideology have little impact upon the way in which the boys saw the world of work? I asked the boys both in the questionnaire and in the interview a question which I felt pushed them fairly hard to express feelings of bitterness towards people who succeeded. 'In Sunderland this year there will be lots of boys leaving school. Why do you think that some of them will get better jobs than yourself?' The question attempted to recreate for the boys a real sense of anger at a situation which they experienced. This appeared to be one of the most 'trying' questions for the boys to answer.

In answering the questionnaire, 29 boys simply answered in terms of 'qualifications' ('They might have 'O' levels, 'A' levels' – *Tom*; 'If they have any certificates' – *Doug*; 'Because they might have G. C. E. or C. S. E.' – *Douglas*; 'Better qualifications' – *Charles P.*). Another 20 mentioned 'O' levels combined with some other factor ('They are more brainy than us and they have better qualifications' – *Frank*; 'They might get better jobs because they might be better with their hands and they might get qualifications' – *Arthur*; 'More 'O' levels and personality' – *Adam*). The next largest category was those that put the capture of better jobs down simply to the boys being more brainy ('They might be more brainy' – *Derek*; 'All depends if you are brainy enough' – *Bruce*). The next category I loosely called working-class cultural explanations ('Because they looked earlier for a job' – *Jimmy*; 'I think they will get a better job because some of their dads will work at the firm what they are going to and their dads will get them a job' – *Fred S.*; 'Because they will be lucky bastards' – *Dick*; 'Because I will not go looking' – *Tim P.*). The rest of the answers ranged individually and widely ('Because they might come from a different school like Bede – *Pat*; 'Some might and some might not get a job' – *Tom P.*; 'No, it should not be right if they get a better job than every other boy' – *Harry*).

All of these answers in some way reflect the experience of the boys and the different ideas with which they have been provided to make sense of the job market. The overwhelming mention of qualifications (49 out of 84 answers) does of course reflect the experiential answer to my question. If any of these boys look at the 'Situations Vacant' column of the *Sunderland Echo*, or if they pick up any of the careers books in the careers room, they immediately see a list of qualifications for a job. Seemingly too, within the boys' own experience, the jobs that ask for the more qualifications are the jobs that provide the most money. Therefore, if some researcher comes along and asks 'Why do some people get better jobs than others?', the answer is obvious – 'qualifications'.

However, the meaning of this answer in terms of the ways in which the boys view the whole structure of the job market is not so simple. For example, the boys could all realise that the best jobs go to those with better qualifications, realise that they had their chance to attain those qualifications and did not, and become angry at missing those chances. Or they could believe that they never had a fair chance to get the qualifications, and that therefore the best jobs were systematically closed to them. Both of these explanations would lead to certain forms of actions.

Yet there is another important set of ideas about qualifications which plays a very important role in the running of the school itself. This is using qualifications as a carrot-and-stick principle to get better behaviour in school. The teacher argues something like this: if you don't behave yourself, you won't work hard; if you don't work hard, then you won't get good qualifications; if you don't get good qualifications, you will get a bad job; if you get a bad job, you won't have much money. Therefore in order to get high wages you have to behave yourself, get good qualifications and so on. In this way it is attempted to maintain order within the school and encourage people to work harder. The high number of boys who mentioned qualifications as the reason for getting a better job would appear to lead us to suppose that this ideology has been successfully transmitted to the boys by their fourth year.

In fact there was one fine example of a boy who had swallowed the whole of this ideology.

Question So you think that the important thing about school is the amount of study that you get in?
Robert Especially for the jobs, as even in the shipyards you need C. S. E.
Question There are lots of boys leaving school in Sunderland this year. They will all be doing different sorts of jobs. Why do you think that some of them will get better jobs than yourself?
Robert Well, some people that leave school might have C. S. E. and some might have nothing. There's only one job that I know where you don't need C. S. E. and that is in a veterinary hospital. All the others you need C. S. E. and G. C. E.

This example backs up the way in which I said boys discovered the job market. Only one job that he knew didn't need qualifications – irrespective of whether this represents the real situation or not, this is the way that this boy makes sense of the thing that we call the labour market. However, if I pushed the simple causal chain in his *own experience* of school, a different picture emerged. I have quoted from this part of an interview before, but it is worth repeating in this context.

Question Why do some boys in Sunderland get better qualifications?
Robert Some boys get better qualifications because they understand the work more easily. Such as in maths, I might be able to get a few right but I can't understand it. It's just the way that different teachers explain it.

Here with this boy there is no feeling that he has, of necessity, to work hard in order to get these qualifications that will lead him to his 'better job'. Indeed, as we have seen, Robert was going into a catering apprenticeship with the Army. He wasn't staying on at school and wanted to leave as soon as possible, without qualifications. The causal chain of work—qualifications—better job, was something which he could see was a description of a reality, but it did not explain HIS world, because Mr Wilson was stuck in mathematical terms so he couldn't have a real chance at all.

In order then to get anywhere near the boys' ideas about the opportunity structure, it was necessary to get at the reasons why people got these better qualifications. The answers that emerged were very simple and completely beyond my expectations.

Question   In Sunderland, why do you think that some of the boys leaving this year will get better jobs?
Jimmy   I dunno. I suppose it's because some of them are swots and that. Some of them don't have toys and that and they stick in on their work at night.
Question   Why do you think that some of the boys in Sunderland will get better qualifications than others?
Jimmy   Most of them are swots and that. They stick in at the work and that. They stay on at school and get good exam marks, while some others like a bit of fun in class and don't bother about school.

This description uncovers some of these boys' ideas about who gets on and who doesn't. It seems to Jimmy that the boys who get better qualifications get better jobs, and the boys who stick in at their work get better qualifications. In this way he describes a simple process he has observed but not one that he feels governs his actions. The question 'Why don't I stick in at my work?' doesn't seem to arise — it's just that other people seem to be able to do it, and I don't. In another case the application of this ideology to the reality of the boy's own life experience was broken by the story of his brother.

Question   Why do some boys get better jobs than yourself?
Eric B.   Might be for qualifications, you never know; some might not get a job at all.
Question   Why will some boys in Sunderland get better qualifications than others?
Eric B.   I don't know . . . my brother took G. C. E. and left school a year later and he couldn't get anywhere. He couldn't even get a job. He's got one now. I'll probably follow in his footsteps to that sort of job.
Question   Are you staying on?
Eric B.   No, I'm going to leave.

Question Lots of boys have said that they might come back to school in September if they havent got a job. Would you do that?
Eric B. No.

Here is a boy whose family experience has cut across and denied the validity of the qualifications ideology, and his own actions would appear to be following the experience rather than the ideology. The fact that some boys appear to be able to work in school and some do not is a thing which these boys seem to have little choice about. You are either a swot or you aren't and nearly all of these are not. The language that they use to talk about this is indicative of this.

Question Why will some boys in Sunderland get better qualifications than others?
Dick Well, some *have* to go out at night and they can't do their homework. They get behind in their work and when they start to revise, sort of thing, they don't revise enough because they haven't got it all there.
Question Are you going to stay on?
Dick I'm leaving at the end of term.

Thus, boys have to go out at night and this stops them from doing their homework. The element of choice about whether you do the work or not is very limited.

Question Why will some boys in Sunderland get better qualifications than others?
Bert I don't know what they do.
Question Well, you know some boys will get 'O' levels and some won't?
Bert Well, you mean some will not get on . . . I think if they stick in at school. Then again some of them are a lot better at learning.
Question Are you leaving?
Bert No, I'm stopping on.
Question What do you want to do?
Bert I haven't thought about it really. It all depends how I do in the exams. If I get real good marks I'll stop on until the sixth. If I get crap ones I'll probably leave.

Bert shows some of the largest element of choice of any of the boys. He may stop on but it depends upon his exam marks; and in a way these are viewed as independent of him. The exam marks will determine whether he is one of the people who are a lot better at learning. The amount of real motivated action left to any of the boys mentioned to date is minimal.

However, the typical explanation of why people get on can best be introduced by a boy who directly quotes the causal-link ideology of hard work—qualifications—more money, but sets it against his own experience and then goes on to show how it is the latter that will determine his action.

Question Why will some boys in Sunderland get better qualifications than others?
Arthur It's because they want a better job and more money and *they must like school 'cos they have to stay on to get better qualifications.*
Question Are you staying on?
Arthur I might but I don't think so.

Arthur brings out the single most important factor about qualifications. In order to get them you have to stay on for them. It is here that the element of choice comes in. In many of the other interviews the answer to the question of why some people get qualifications is simply because they stay on at school. Experientially, the boys can see that those who do stay on at school an extra voluntary year *do* get C. S. E. and G. C. E., and it is this experience that they were relating to me.

Question Why will some boys leaving school in Sunderland get better qualifications than others?
Dave Probably because they stay on another year, and don't like to gang out with lads who are working.
Question Why will some boys . . . better qualifications than others?
William 'Cos most of them stop on until their fifth year.
Question Why will some boys . . . better qualifications than others?
Tom Because they wanted to stay on and get better qualifications.

Thus, given that the boys seem to recognise that better qualifications lead to better jobs in a much simpler way than educationalists might, why then don't they take this opportunity for better jobs by simply staying on at school for that extra year. They paint a simple picture of better opportunities and then do not avail themselves of it. All of these lads, though, recognise that you only stay on at school if you have a certain favourable relationship with that institution. If you experience it as an institution where you work and learn, then it is possible to stay on, but for most of these boys there is no chance of staying on. They experience the school as attacking them; they feel it is not possible to spend another year there. Thus they have no real hesitation in refusing the inevitable 'better job' and leaving as soon as they can. Another boy put an even more sensitive analysis of how staying on caused better qualifications.

Question Why will some boys leaving school in Sunderland get better qualifications than others?
Edward Well, like it's just because they stay on at school. Then they take more interest in school and they get more qualifications and all this.
Question Are you staying on at all?
Edward No, I'm leaving.

Edward puts forward the idea that staying on that extra year at school actually changes the quality of the relationship between the boy and the education system. If you stay on, the investment of time and energy will change the boy's view of the work process, and he will become more committed and therefore more interested, and therefore his work will improve and he will attain qualifications.

However, this once more remains at the level of a description of others' actions, not a prescription for his own.

In this way, the boys saw the attainment of better qualifications NOT as a result of a greater innate intelligence, but simply as a reward for staying power. Their own reasons for their own lack of attainment are equally simple – they couldn't stick it for another year or two.

The discussion of better qualifications sprung from the boys seeing that as the pathway to better jobs. Many of them, though, had much more culturally-tied answers as to why people got better jobs.

Question In Sunderland, why do you think that some of the boys leaving this year will get better jobs than you?
Edward Sometimes it's because their dad gets them in because they know the head man and that.
Question In Sunderland, why . . . get better jobs than you?
Dick Some lads have their father in the job and he is a big influence in the job and he will put a word in, and they might be daft as a post, but they will still get a good job.

s.s.s.k.—G

Neither of these boys had any personal experience of influence in finding somebody a job, but another had:

Question In Sunderland, why . . . get better jobs than you?
Arthur 'Cos they might be more brainier and their fathers might already have their name down and their fathers might have a good job at the firm that they've wanted. Or they've got friends. 'Cos my friend, like, his dad's one of the best friends of the foreman and he is going to get my mate a job already.

Here we have the description of the opportunity structure as actually experienced by these boys. None of the boys actually said that it was 'unfair' that some boys' dads had influence and some did not. This was accepted as part of the many obvious inevitabilities of working-class youth, without anger and expressed frustration.

However, the single biggest explanation given by the boys as to how they reckon to get better or worse jobs can be labelled quite simply 'vigilance'. The important factor about getting better jobs is the proximity of the person looking to the vagaries of the market. It is here again that a limited form of choice enters into the ideology of the opportunity structure.

Question In Sunderland, why do you think that some of the boys leaving this year will get better jobs than you?
Derek I dunno. They might prepare things before they leave. You know, go around before they leave and have everything ready 'cos if you don't do that you always just have to get the job that comes.
Question In Sunderland, why . . . get better jobs than you?
Frank It's because some people just don't care what sort of a job that they get. Or they might get a teaboy's job or something like that and they say, 'Well I've got a job and I'm sticking to that until I get the sack' and they just go on like that. It's a bad life really, but the others, who go out searching for good jobs, if *they* get that job I think they would not be satisfied and they would go on until they were satisfied.

Basically, then, if you look early and you simply keep on looking, then you get the better jobs; whereas if you look late and give up, then you get the worse jobs. This attitude both reflects the historical experience of the working class towards their opportunity structure, and also mirrors the boys' actual experience of the labour market. Historically, if you wanted a job at all in times of unemployment, then you needed to be in constant touch with the Labour Exchange, and to keep reading the 'Situations Vacant' column in the daily newspapers, and to keep going round to work places where there might be vacancies. Unless you did this you either ended up unemployed or simply got the worse job. This is the dominant message that the boys' background gives them. It is confirmed by their experience:

Question In Sunderland, why . . . get better jobs than you?
Bert There's a lad called Rick Stonley who didn't bother going down the Youth Employment or watching the papers to see what jobs were in. He just didn't want a job. Some of them are going and trying to get a job all the time.

In this vigilance towards the labour market, though, there are some boys that start out with a perceived advantage. These are not the boys who went to the better schools, but simply those who were born between September and April and can therefore choose to leave at Easter. In real terms these boys have an advantage over those who leave in July. As one boy patiently explained to me:

Steven Some will be looking at Easter and they've got time to get a job whereas when the main batch leave in the summer there will be five pople going after each job.

This then is the experiential reality of the opportunity structure for these boys. At no stage in either the interviews or the questionnaire do they reach out from their class backgrounds and use a comparison that comes from outside. There are no comparisons at all with boys who go on to university or become bank managers or take any other form of middle-class employment. Whilst all the questions are deliberately phrased to include comparison with *everyone* in Sunderland, *all* the answers are phrased in terms of the working class of Sunderland. This brings into question a whole range of ideas, not only those of sociologists, but also a much wider set of commonsense ideas about the breakdown of class barriers.

Not only is there no direct comparison by these boys between their jobs and the jobs of people outside their experience, but there is no application of an ideology of opportunity structure that comes from outside their experience of the labour market. Any notion of 'egalitarian' ideology is never referred to. These boys' worlds are ordered by experientially tried and tested means of understanding the world, even though these may appear 'irrational' to the outside observer.

The changeover from school to work is also very different from the picture previously painted; the boys don't see their world in terms of choice and career; when the job comes it comes in a harsh and real form. It shares certain things with school; you have to go and it's boring. However, the one difference between school and work is that you can opt out of that particular job in the hope that things will be different; you can opt for a specific series of temporary changes. This is a characteristic of my impressions of these boys' elder brothers. They change jobs very quickly; have periods of temporary unemployment; get another job; can't stand it and leave. This constant change continues until they find a job which they can't leave, like the Army, or one that isn't as bad or has compensations. It all ends anyway when you get married; then you have to keep the job you're in, hate it or not.

School, work and society

Some of the major issues that have been discussed in the Great Education Debate since October 1976 will be outlined later in the conclusions; here, however, it is important to relate this chapter to the question of the way in which school relates to industrial training. Much of what these boys said would lead me to say that the whole debate is wrongly founded. The children do feel that school should relate to their future world of work; they see this world as one that is full of boredom and insecurity, NOT full of adventure and choice. The liberal mode of education which tries to foster their 'leisure interests' is irrelevant to them; but the direct teaching of qualifications that lead to work is also not seen as possible for most of the boys. This latter alternative is not open to them since the role of exams and qualifications has a control function within the school which the boys react against. Thus the relationship between 'industry and education' is incorrectly posed through either education for training or education for work. This will be followed up later.

5

What do they get out of pop music and football?

So far I have looked at the boys' reactions to school. For the most part they may have appeared valid; yet their ideas and values have been entirely viewed as a *response*. As such it may well occur to readers that there is nothing positive in the culture that the boys are trying to protect. If this were indeed the case their struggle to protect themselves at school would be very difficult. However, in the next two chapters I will try to outline the positive aspects of their lives in their own terms. When I started the research I had wanted to centre as much as possible upon their school experiences. It is once more an example of the necessarily messy approach to research that I had to depart from this focus. 14-year-old boys did not live their lives in one institution; they listened to pop music; went to football matches; hung about on street corners.

In looking beyond the school it became possible to see very clearly the ways in which the conflict that I have outlined as taking place within the school continued outside it. For whilst the boys had reacted against the school's positive culture, so did the school react against that of the boys. The structure of the boys' leisure activities turned out to be as antipathetic to the school as the school's structure had been antipathetic to the boys. These mutual antipathies were very important, since I quickly learnt that education as a process goes on all the time for these boys; and the antipathies betrayed two very different sorts of 'education' and learning going on in these boys' lives. It became vital for me to try to understand the nature of the ideas and values learnt at football and on the street.

Therefore this chapter represents an attempt to talk to the boys about pop music and football; the next is about their street-based activities. The leisure activities of adolescent working-class male youth can be seen as one of the major continuing obsessions of social democracy in the western world. Not only are the general lines of each new form of activity chronicled by the media, but the specifics of the length of hair, type of violence, nature of the crime and style of clothes have been leapt upon with all the glee of the intelligent bourgeois Victorian attending the latest lecture on a new African tribe.

Sociology, with it's ever-faithful role of attempting to render intelligible these problems, has also attempted to come to grips with what these boys do in their spare time. Indeed, I was no exception to this quest; it was specifically with the links between secondary education and juvenile delinquency that I had started my research. Consequently much of my time was spent in understanding how these boys got into trouble with the law; such an understanding was obviously impossible without coming to grips with their whole range of leisure activities. Thus in trying to see why they bashed up telephone boxes, it was important to see the context of their Saturday evenings. Any discussion of adolescent male leisure activities in the north-east must revolve around football and pop music. So the next two chapters must be seen as attempting to talk about getting into trouble within the context of the whole of their spare-time activities.

How has sociology made sense of kids' spare-time activities?

There has been no coherent theoretical attempt to provide us with a way of thinking about rule-breaking activity as a part of a wider leisure activity of young people. Within sociology there have been a number of attempted sophistications of this position, all of which were of importance to my original understanding of the problems I was confronting in Sunderland. All of these theories rested at least in part upon the twin concepts of 'leisure activities' and 'delinquency'.

Leisure

Leisure activities have been seen quite simply as those activities engaged in outside 'work'. This concept has been used in a variety of ways, all of which tend to diminish class differentiations. Whilst it is obvious, the argument runs, that there are still differences in the field of work between the classes, and that such differences can be seen within other fields such as educational facilities, such differences *disappear* in people's leisure. Thus everyone now goes out to dinner, everyone goes for a drink, everyone goes for a drive at weekends and, amongst young people, everyone follows the same football clubs and the same pop groups.

Such a belief is important in studying young people since it becomes assumed that all youths experience similar activities outlined above in the same way. This makes the problem for the researcher a fairly simple one: all he has to do is discover which of the activities the groups of youths he is looking at take part in, and which they don't like. It becomes a matter of giving the boys a checklist and asking them to tick off the requisite ones, which is indeed something I did.

Delinquency

Within sociology recent years have seen what appears to be a complete change in the way that deviance is thought about. Sociologists have begun to try and see such behaviour within the context of the people concerned, rather than as a set of activities which are self-evidently 'wrong'. They have begun to ask questions, not only about who breaks rules, but also about who makes them. Such questions have led away from the more individualistic searching for the single characteristic that sorts out rule-breakers from the others. Much of research in the 1950s and 1960s had specifically looked at individual rule-breakers as a group radically different from others. This was especially true in the field of juvenile delinquency, where the search for variables became tied to the social importance of isolating offenders at as young an age as possible. If it were possible to isolate future offenders early, it would be possible to 'cure' them before they began their delinquent activities. Such an approach, though, was severely attacked by a whole plethora of self-report delinquency surveys.

These surveys consist of asking people if they have ever committed any of a list of likely offences from shoplifting and joyriding up to grievous bodily harm. The number of respondents who admitted breaking some or other laws when they were young was always very high. Such a response showed that offences against laws were not simply caused by one characteristic or another; rather they were the result of a series of age-related experiences.

This and other evidence created an atmosphere where research into juvenile delinquency had to become closely linked with research into youth culture; where the predominant focus of the research changed from the individual law-breaker and his law-breaking activities to the overall set of activities carried out in the youth's spare time. It was here that my research initially focused.

Blocked leisure opportunities

In the last chapter I mentioned the ideas about the frustrations of working-class boys at their continued inability to get on in a middle-class world. I believed that these frustrations built up around the difficulties of getting on in the fields of school and work. I also believed this to be true in the field of leisure activities.

Given these difficulties of making it in the work field it is likely that working-class boys will get their status from their leisure, and that such activities and status have a differential importance for middle-class kids since they get some satisfaction from their school activities. However, since working-class kids have less financial resources than their middle-class counterparts, they find that certain leisure opportunities are denied them. Thus they suffer a double deprivation leading to a double frustration. David Downes in studying adolescents in east London puts much faith upon these ideas:

> There is some reason to suppose, however, that the working class corner boy both lays greater stress on its leisure goals, and has far less legitimate access to them, than male adolescents differentially placed in the social structure. This discrepancy is thought to be enough to provide immediate impetus to a great deal of group delinquency, limited in ferocity but diversified in content. [1]

So in looking at spare-time activities in Sunderland I would expect the boys to be greatly distressed at their lack of attainment in the field of leisure status.

Teenage culture

The existence of teenage culture since the middle 1950s has completely changed the way in which sociologists think about young people. It has been widely believed that this culture has been received by all the teenagers in equal amounts; that such a thing as a teenage culture exists over and above any class differences. Such ideas have been further supplemented by the whole debate about generational conflict.

Teenage culture has been seen as an all-encompasing blanket

process. The boys in Sunderland and the 24-year-old Kings Roader in Chelsea experience this culture in the same way. This is believed because teenage culture is viewed as completely synthetic culture which is created *for* and not *by* teenagers. The culture is seen as created specifically for an economic market – that is, working-class males between 15 and 25 initially, who were the original group with the time and money – that it was possible to exploit. Teenagers outside this group are affected by the culture even though it was not created for them.

The late 1960s saw the emergence of a series of economic markets which were further exploited. These different markets see developing different parts of that culture; most obviously, the expansion of the student market following the Robbins Report represents a very different set of music and styles from the working-class male rocker or mod.

The single most important factor about the ways in which I viewed teenage culture was the fact that it was created *for* rather than *by* working-class kids.

Talking to the kids about their spare-time activities

Most of this preceding discussion would lead me to categorise working class spare-time behaviour in terms of the legal/non-legal or leisure/non-leisure activities. Immediately, though, in talking with the boys I found these categories had very little meaning in their own experience of spare-time activity. In this chapter I have tried to separate out those activities which boys take part in inside organisations, since these represent specific sorts of experiences to do with the ways in which I misperceived their culture. I have further split these 'organised' activities into two very different kinds of organisational settings: firstly, there are a series of organisations which deal with young people and are aimed specifically at trying to change these people in some way; secondly, there are those organisations which are set up to make money and into which young people *buy* their entry. The first organisation is based upon the youth club idea, yet does not exclude others (for example, those linked with school, such as school music and football).

The other group deals with commercial bodies which are based upon football and pop music; the boys take part in these and are controlled by them in an entirely different way from the first group. It is interesting to see these categories of activities from another point of view and to recognise the great similarity between my categories and those of the magistrate. Whilst in the north-east visits to juvenile courts saw magistrate after magistrate exhorting young offender, probation officer, parent and the press to attempt to get young people involved in 'structured leisure activities'. These activities almost exactly fitted my first category of spare-time activity. The bench looked with some disfavour upon youths' involvement with commercial activities; and with very great distaste upon any involvement with the street.

Structured leisure activities

The amount that the boys were involved in activities which are adult-regulated was very small. Such organisations have been styled by social scientists in the past as 'like the white corpuscles of the blood stream, attacking infection and minimising the source of danger to the body as a whole'[2] and for the vast majority of the boys that I got to know in Sunderland these corpuscles had no significance at all. Like the school itself, like the education system as a whole, like the Duke of Edinburgh Award Scheme, like the scouts, like the Youth Service and like school-based leisure activities, the youth clubs in the area would all describe themselves as non-authoritarian. They would describe themselves and their organisation in terms of client organisations – that is, based as much as possible upon the individual child. None of these organisations would describe themselves as either 'authoritarian' or based upon anything but trying to build up the character of the children. This self-image becomes important when we try to make sense of the boys' perceptions, since it accentuates the gap in perception between individuals who run these pastimes and the kids involved. An example of this was the Duke of Edinburgh Award Scheme run in Municipal School. This is a scheme that is supposed to have a large degree of 'choice' for the boys in its content and to get individual boys away from their environment; that is, in short, to attract fairly tough individuals who 'want a challenge'. However, the teacher in charge of this activity at the school was the one teacher who, it was universally agreed by all the boys, 'took fits' and hit people with stools. To the people who organised the activity in the school it must have seemed strange that none of the boys who could have gained from the activity ever took part, yet it is significant that any of these boys could themselves have told them that the master was significantly disliked. This is not to say that if another master was in charge all the boys would have gained a bronze award, but it shows the gap between the controllers of the activities and the boys; a gap sufficiently big to stop nearly all the boys from taking part.

In the field of their experience of youth clubs the differences in the type of control experienced by the boys is directly related to the aims that the institution may have, and to what they are trying to do 'with' or 'for' the boy. The difficulties of, say, the youth club are immense in that they are trying to change the boys' attitudes and behaviour, yet do not have the compulsory powers of attendance that the school 'enjoys'.

This is reflected in one boy's reaction to the youth club:

Question   Would you tell me what you do on an average Saturday evening?
Roland   We used to go down the youth club, but now we stay on the streets.
Question   Why did you leave the youth club?
Roland   They were telling us what to do and that ain't fair.
Question   Why not?
Roland   They can't tell us what to do.

Here is a very strong echo of the boys' attitudes towards school, with the one vital proviso that they do not *have* to go to youth clubs. So they try out the youth clubs, and from many clubs there is a beckoning freedom; yet this freedom is soon contradicted, when the youth leader labels certain forms of behaviour as dangerous or aimless, when violence becomes discouraged as an unstructured leisure activity. As soon as any of the boys engage in those activities they are 'told what to do'. As a consequence the boys leave the youth club and, unless they take the options outlined at the beginning of the next chapter, never see the institution again.

Running throughout the boys' spare-time activities is the game of football. Half the boys said that they played football every day, and only seven never played at all. We are told by most football commentators that the game of football is the same, from kicking the ball around the back streets of Barnsley to the 'lush green turf of Wembley'. Yet these boys showed that this similarity was there in name only—not in experience. It is specifically the *mode* of organisation of the sport that is important; it is this which creates the different sorts of experience of the boys. In the case of playing football for the school there is the most obvious difference in the organisation. Sociologists in the past have commented upon boys' reluctance to play sports for the school:

> On the question of sport most of the teachers believed that it was the boys with superior academic performance who made the best sportsmen. Whilst it is true that there tends to be a low positive correlation between intelligence and skill at games, the disproportionate representation of high stream boys in sporting activities takes no account of the fact that low stream norms reduce motivation both to achieve academically and to participate in extra-curricular activities, especially when these are associated with loyalty to the school. This point may be illustrated. On one occasion during an informal discussion with Derek of 4D I learned that he was going to the swimming baths after school. I also discovered that such visits were a regular event for Derek and some of his friends, and that they were fairly able swimmers. When I asked Derek for which events he would enter in the School Swimming Gala he retorted: 'I wouldn't swim for the bloody school.'[3]

In this way sociologists have attempted to explain why boys don't go in for school sports. The boys who don't go into the school teams and have got the skill reject their place because they feel that they would not like to be seen colluding with the school authorities. In talking to the boys in Sunderland I found that it was not a simple wish to be seen as dissociating yourself from the school, rather it was a dislike of the *mode* of sport. Hargreaves tells us that Derek was a 'fairly able' swimmer, but what exactly does this mean? That he can swim a certain distance in a certain time? That he has a beautiful style? That he can swim for miles? From what I gathered from the realms of playing footy, the kids would feel that 'going swimming with their mates' represents a different sort of experience from 'swimming for the school'. The latter is a highly structured experience, where you HAVE to turn up at a certain time, you have to swim at a certain time, in a certain style, in a certain lane, and equally important you have to stop at a certain time. The enterprise is massively *structured* in its entirety; and when compared to going down to the pool and having a few races with your mates, is a completely different experience.

School sports are not simply an attempt to allow the boys a chance to enjoy themselves, they are meant to instil a certain attitude to sports as their prime reason for being on the timetable. Playing football for the school represents a certain form of 'playing football' which by no means represents the 'normal' way of playing football for the boys in this study.

Indeed, this point was clarified for me by two boys who had specifically given up playing football for the school, even though they enjoyed the game. This was done primarily because they couldn't maintain their enthusiasm for the activity *despite* the imposed structure.

Question Do you like football?
Bert Yes, a lot. I used to play for the school team only you had to turn out every Saturday, and you had to buy a bag so I dropped out.
Question Where do you play football around here?
Bert Used to play outside the metalwork shop. But the coppers came and said 'Next time we catch you here you're gonna get summoned'. He took the ball away in his panda.

This illustrates the different nature of the games involved. As far as the Football League is concerned the dangers of the game are only an injury or two, or perhaps an attack of cramp in extra time; for the boys it varies from having to buy a bag to dodging the police, depending on the sort of game being played.

Question Do you play football?
Steven Yes, it's great. I played for the school team but they wanted you out every Saturday whatever the weather. Playing in rain and cold and snow. It's no fun playing that way. So I dropped out.

Both of these boys didn't like to turn out every Saturday to play for the school. The structured, organised way of playing the game was not at all their way of playing. It was not that they did not express enthusiasm for the game; rather that a *specific sort* of game failed to attract their enthusiasm. It was just that (to put it succinctly) playing football for the school is not *their* game.

To underline the way in which the different structure of the different ways of playing football affected different boys, I interviewed two boys who found that playing football for the school reflected *their* way of playing football. They felt that football was about a structured game with individual skills.

These two boys (Fred S. and Billy) said that they disliked school, and indeed that they came to school because they liked playing football for the school.

Question   Do you play football?
Fred S.   Yes, I play for the school. I'm good at it and enjoy playing football against good opposition.

Question   Do you play football?
Billy   Aye, every chance that I can get. For the school too. Nothing like a really good game with all the gear. I'm fast on the wing you know.

Both lads play the sort of football that is highly enjoyable in an organised, eleven-a-side, 45-minutes-each-half sort of game. They enjoy exercising their individual skill at the game and, as George Best would testify, the expression of individual skill is easier in a structured game with a well-defined set of rules and a hard referee.

It was possible to play football in a structured way outside the school. One boy (Robert), who talked about his father and him doing everything together and who wanted to join the Army, said that he didn't like playing football, but enjoyed being a referee or a linesman.

Robert   Well, it's just that I certainly understand the game a bit more when I am refereeing. Up until now I have run on the line for a couple of clubs like Smithfield Men's Club. I've run on the line for them for about four times. I think it's a lot more exciting on the line because you can understand the game a bit more and you can decide decisions.

For this boy, football represents a game of rules to understand, a picture which fits much more snugly into the commonsense idea of what football is.

I have attempted to show that, for these boys, there are a number of different games of football, rather than one game with one label. For most of them the activity of playing football was not that of the structured game.

Music and school culture

The advent of pop music has changed the ways in which adults view young people's music, and now there is at least a recognition if not a tolerance of a fairly wide range of music. This change has affected teachers too. Nevertheless, nearly all schools have some form of orchestra which represents the school at functions and this orchestra has to reflect a more traditional form of music. Consequently pressure is applied on pupils in most schools to join school orchestras and choirs; and few schools organise their own pop groups. In the north-east the traditional school orchestra is not one that necessarily includes strings; rather it is based upon the model of a brass band. Other adult organised institutions that the boys came into contact with also organised their music on the basis of an orchestra or band — such as the Salvation Army and the Boy's Brigade. The same was true of choirs either inside or outside the school or the church. Thus for these 14-year-olds any actual activity in the field of music must be in an adult organised institution of a non-pop variety. The only cases of boys taking an active part in this type of music were two boys who played instruments in bands.

Question Do you like pop music?
Frank A bit, but I play in the school orchestra, you know, and I'm in a local orchestra, the Sunderland Youth Orchestra. I take a good interest in that and it's held on Friday nights.

Question What do you do with your spare time?
Harry I play in the Salvation Army band.
Question What's it like?
Harry I'm going to give it up when I leave school. I like playing trombone, like, but I don't like the band.

No boys sung in any choir, either school or church. These two boys played in these bands despite their structure, rather than because of it. If you're 'good at the trombone' then that's the only opportunity of playing it. The effect of structure upon the boys' feeling for music is expressed by discussing the school band's show put on for parents and friends at Municipal School in the summer term of 1970.

The concert consisted of three parts: music played by the band; music sung by the band and choir; and a 'sing-song' in which everyone joined.

In the first two sessions the band played adequately and with great precision. The music master made jokes about composers' names like Greig and the music consisted of light classical themes. Each number was enthusiastically applauded by the teachers and their friends in the first three rows (see diagram); however, the rest of the audience seemed a bit bored, talking through the pieces and so on. In the choral pieces, the choir stood stiffly to attention and breathed massively in and out as taught by music teachers everywhere. Teachers were very proud of the occasion and I heard them say 'how very good the children were', 'how well behaved'.

At the end of this part of the concert, however, a duplicated sheet of songs of a 'sing-song' variety was handed out. Directly the drummer started off the rhythm section of the orchestra in the first number, all the music master's attempts to encourage participation by the audience were seen to be superfluous. Everyone behind the first three rows became animated and were belting out 'Way down Swanee'. By the second number, 'I'm forever blowing bubbles', the orchestra had changed completely in tone and the choir began spontaneously clapping on the beat. At this stage the music master had become a useless appendage. The boys and girls had seen their parents get into the situation (remember they were facing them across three rows of teachers) and then became involved themselves; this involvement fired their parents even more.

The teachers, on the other hand, reacted as the music master expected the parents to react: with an initial nervousness about singing, and more nervousness about being in the middle of two sets of singing people who were behaving as if they were in the club on a Saturday night. As one teacher remarked in the staff room next morning, 'There was no need for that singing, it ruined the whole concert'. What does this mean in terms of the boys' experiences of music? It shows that usually the music as experienced at school bears little relationship to the music that they experience at home. Whilst the 'sing-song' music was not teenage music ('I'm forever blowing bubbles' is not 'I can't get no satisfaction') it was experienced as 'pop'. Thus when only 15 per cent of the boys said that their parents disliked pop music, it was this sort of music that they were talking about.

This concert had implications for any general understanding of the structure of spare-time activity, for the structures within this concert were changed *directly* the content had changed from that which was normal in a school concert. The school concert structure would not withstand the pressure of being turned into, for a while, a club 'sing-song'. Whilst this structure was under attack, the whole experience for the pupils changed dramatically. What, then, is it possible to say

Orchestra

Choir

Music master

Teachers and friends

Parents and brothers and sisters

Plan of school band show

about the boys' experiences of structured leisure activities? Firstly, and most obviously, very few boys took part in them. Secondly, the reason for this was generally because of the *structure* of such activities. They were organised in such a way that the boys did not feel at home with them. They were likened to school activities, yet they did not have the compulsion of school. Consequently they were ignored. Thirdly, different structures in the field of music and football, structures organised by the kids themselves, where they didn't feel that people were trying to change them, were acceptable.

Commercial organisations

Pop music

It is interesting if we turn from looking at the school concert to the boys' attitudes to their own music, pop music. Whilst I have never felt competent to analyse the deep meaning of pop music for these boys (or indeed for myself since I *do* find that I 'just like the beat') it is easy to see it as important to them. As I have said before, much of the sociology has oversimplified some of the complex relationships involved. Pop music has an existence for all these boys, not simply those who went to dance halls.

This music has a meaning and is important to young people both as a series of discrete sounds (singles, L. P.s, radio shows) and as a total genre. That is, each boy has a relationship not only with, for example, the Beatles as a group, but with pop music as a whole. Similarly, the boys relate to these two phenomena (that is, the performer as an individual and the genre as a whole) not only as themselves as individuals but as part of *their* group too, which might either be confined to the street corner or be their whole generation.

Thus the relationship of youth with pop music is complex in terms of who exactly is relating to whom. For example:

Youth	Pop music
Individual boy	Individual 'sound'
Small group	Group's music as a whole
General group	Pop music as a whole

This is more than simply a neat pattern of categories; it represents an attempt to explain some massive and apparently misunderstood relationships between experience and musical constructs.

Thus it is not sufficient simply to show the answers to the question of whether the boys liked pop music:

Favourable responses	70	(Great; fab; groovy, baby, groovy; fuckin' hellish)
Uncommitted	9	(All right; okay)
Disliked	9	(Bloody horrible; silly)

This does show some relationship between the boys and pop music as a whole. Similarly boys were asked, 'Do your friends like pop music?' 80 said yes and nine said no. From both these questions it appears possible to say definitely that the boys and their friends like pop music. Whilst this is self-evidently true, what it means is something very different because boys actually *experience* the cultural construct of pop music very differently and define what pop music is very differently.

On an individual level the relationship between the boy and his five favourite pop groups/stars represented one of the most inexplicable parts of the whole research. As has been said before, there was *no* significant difference between the two schools in any of the areas of overall interest, or indeed in any of the separate questions, with the single exception of the two schools' selection of their five favourite pop groups/stars. Thus in Municipal Comprehensive School this was the boys' selection:

21	Deep Purple
15	Led Zeppelin
13	Free
10	Jimi Hendrix, Black Sabbath
9	Beatles
7	Herman's Hermits
6	The Who
5	T. Rex
4	Elvis Presley, Desmond Dekker, C. C. S., Family, Bob Dylan
3	Tom Jones, Jethro Tull, Blue Mink, Tremeloes, Edwin Starr, Dave Clark Five, Groundhogs
2	Mary Hopkin, Cream, Andy Williams, Mungo Jerry, Canned Heat, Captain Beefheart, Bee Gees, Pickety Witch, Tamla Motown
1	Monkees
6	None

These choices could be characterised as 'hard rock' choices, 59 votes being cast for the five favourite pop groups, all of which are characterised by a driving-beat kind of music. Indeed, Herman's Hermits is the only group receiving more than four votes which has not at some time played hard rock music. In December 1970, when this survey was made, the list reads like a who's who of hard rock.

However, looking at the choices made by Cunningham Secondary Modern School, a very different picture emerges. One that is far less tightly classifiable, and is possibly *only* classifiable by the absence of hard rock music:

15 Beatles
13 Tom Jones
11 Elvis Presley
7 Cliff Richard
6 Herman's Hermits, Hollies, Rolling Stones
5 Freddie and the Dreamers
4 Monkees, C. C. S., Free
3 Deep Purple, Jethro Tull, Engelbert Humperdinck,
   The Who, Tremeloes, Ten Years After, Cream
2 Des O'Connor, Shadows, Val Doonican, Scaffold,
   Shirley Bassey, Frank Sinatra, Led Zeppelin
1 Moody Blues
10 None

To any aficionado of pop music in 1970 this list has a particularly *déjà vu* look about it; it seems to lack any of the new groups in the Municipal School choices.

Yet both groups of boys 'like pop music', both groups of boys define their friends as 'liking pop music', both groups of boys listen to records and watch *Top of the Pops* to the same extent; both are as likely or unlikely to read magazines about pop music. The only set of meanings that I can concretely deduce from this is that the concept of 'pop music' is *very* diffuse as far as working-class youth is concerned. You *can* watch *Top of the Pops* for either the Tom Jones – Elvis Presley–Cliff Richard axis or the Deep Purple–Led Zeppelin–Free axis and see in it a good programme. For it is in the nature of the 'pop music' institution, such as Jimmy Saville and *Top of the Pops*, to try and please as large a group as possible of young people.

Unfortunately it is very difficult to say anything more positive about pop music as a cultural experience for the boys. The nature of the research was not sufficiently sensitive to this area to be able to say what, for example, driving rock means to those boys who like it, or what it means to those who don't like it. I feel that I can only say something general about the musical experience of these boys and of its importance. It does seem to be quite important as an atmosphere-maker rather than as something that you listen to attentively. Unlike football it is not a subject that is talked about; 'Did you hear the latest single?' is not as common as 'Did you see Macdonald's goal on *Match of the Day*?' In fact, talking about pop music did not seem to crop up at all in activities, but talking about football did a lot.

Question Do you listen to pop music?

Wyn All the time.

Question At home?

Wyn On the radio. I can't see it on a Thursday night, because I'm down the club on a Thursday.

Question Do you ever go to a place where there is a juke box?

Wyn We go to the Mecca on Sunday and sometimes we go to cafes with me mates sometimes.

Thus this interview allows the researcher to say that the boy expresses great interest in pop music (his five favourite pop groups were the Beatles, Deep Purple, Black Sabbath, The Who and Led Zeppelin) and that he spends quite a lot of time involved in activities concerned with pop music. But it does not allow me to say anything about the meaning of the groups or the records for him. It is on this deeper level that a cultural analysis of the meanings of music must be carried out.

Whilst it may be very difficult to speak with any certainty about the deeper meaning of individual sets of music to the boys, it did become clear that there was a set of experiences which could be talked about, and this was going to a pop concert and going to a dance hall. Obviously such experiences are linked with the nature of the music (the differences between rock concerts, folk concerts and jazz concerts do relate to the music, though they are never totally *caused* by it) but they do not necessarily spring totally from it. The rock concert and the dance hall represent somewhere to go for those who not only enjoy pop music but want something else too.

Question Do you listen to much pop music?

Ian Well, I stay in on a Thursday night to watch *Top of the Pops*. Then I'm back on the streets again about half-past-eight.

Question Do you ever go down the Mecca?

Ian Well, I used to go down the Rank on a Saturday night but I used to get into trouble so I stopped going.

Question Do you and your mates listen to pop music when you go round each other's homes?

William Aye, we've got all the L. P.s.

Question Do you go down the Mecca?

William No. We get kicked around by the skinheads.

Question Don't they have special nights with skinhead sort of music?

William No, they're down there all the time.

So the dance halls are not simply places where music is played, but where fights and trouble take place. Not surprisingly, the fights and the troubles become more important than the music, even though both of the boys specify their interest in other ways of listening to music.

For others, the dance hall provides *both* a place to listen to music and a place either to chat up the lasses or to have a fight. These boys seem very committed to pop music of a specific kind and in fact they would appear to be using the dance hall in a very different way.

Question What do you do on an average Saturday evening?
Bert Don't usually go out on a Saturday. Go out on a Sunday. Last Sunday we went down the Mecca and saw The Free and Amazing Blondel.
Question Do you and your mates go down there every Sunday?
Bert Yes.
Question What do you do down there?
Bert Listen to the music and chat up the lasses.
Question Do you ever get involved in any kind of trouble?
Bert Sometimes with a couple of skins. Sometimes when the skins come we have a scrap . . . sometimes.

Question Do you like pop music?
Doug It's hellish great.
Question Where do you listen to it?
Doug On telly, but we go down the Mecca on Tuesday. Tuesdays they have special music for skins.
Question Why?
Doug Well, they don't let us in other nights. Any case, the music is best on a Tuesday, and the lasses too.

These boys seem a lot more selective about using the institution of dance halls. In a way, they are pushing the autonomy of the buyer in the cash-nexus situation as far as possible. They say we are here not only for the music that you offer us, but also for the social institutions that we can create out of the freedom that we are allowed. We come for the music that you sell us AND we come for the lasses and the trouble that we can make.

All these impressions of the importance of these group experiences can be backed up by any visit to a rock concert. In really trying to come to grips with this aspect of the kids' lives I went to a number of rock concerts in different parts of the country (well, also because I enjoy going to rock concerts!) The most striking example of the experience was in visiting a Slade concert in Earls Court. Slade only became a national group after I had finished my research, but it would seem likely that to the kids at Municipal School, at any rate, they would have represented their favourite group. The experience of this concert, though, starts long before the music starts; long before you enter the hall; for when I joined the District Line tube train at Sloane Square I was already among the pop crowd. My immediate impression was confused because the train was full of West Ham fans decked out in scarves, rosettes, and occasionally singing 'I'm forever blowing bubbles'. Being a West Ham fan there seemed nothing odd about this except that the District Line train was heading in the wrong direction, it was a Sunday evening and several of the fans had large top hats with silver circles pasted on them (the hat that the lead singer of the Slade, Noddy Holder, wears). This immediate impression of a football crowd became more significant at Earls Court; here the Shed from Chelsea, the North Bank from Arsenal, the Rough End from Spurs, Millwall and even Fulham were all massed in one space. It then became the quintessential London teenage football crowd. The music and the audience participation made this all the more obvious; it was a football crowd with no game. The experience of going to this concert obviously *depended* upon the Slade playing their music (as any Slade fan will agree); but the concert was a total group experience of a certain kind that went on both before and after the music.

Therefore, when we try and make sense of rock music for teenagers it does nothing simply to try to understand the music itself; it must be seen as relating to a whole range of working-class group experiences many of which are outside the music itself and all of which are a group-experienced phenomenon.

Football

This can be directly linked with the nature of the experience of going to a football match; indeed, the connection is made by the media in their continuing discussion of the 'rising tide of violence'.

Over the past few years there have been claims about the increasing violence by teenagers both at dance halls and football matches. But the question arises of whether this violence IS actually increasing or, as is more likely, there is now a different sort of experience involved.

What *is* violence at football matches and dance halls?

Question   Do you watch much football?
Derek M.   We chant, have a scrap with some of the lads. Perhaps have a crack at other supporters. Keep away from coppers. Watch the match too (laughs).
Question   Do you get into trouble?
Derek M.   Aye, but not real trouble and it's great.

Football is being offered to these boys by Sunderland F. C., or rather the right to stand and watch a football match and to shout for Sunderland. Rather than simply accept that, they take part in a complete and different set of experiences called 'going to footy'. This *includes* watching the football, and in fact is pervaded throughout by what is happening on the field in front of them,* but is a collection of experiences that are not simply watching a game of soccer. Such experiences are difficult for me to articulate, let alone the boys. To be at your team's ground in the middle of a good game of football is *more* than watching a game of soccer. To go with your mates to the Fulwell End is to take part in a collective and creative experience that starts at about half-past-one and finishes at about six o'clock. This experience may lead to violence either of a verbal (chanting) or of a physical character, but is not *necessarily* an experience characterised by violence.

Similarly in a dance hall. The music, like the football, pervades the experience but does not limit that experience to a spectator one. Taylor has written historically about the fan attempting to recapture control of his game;[4] and my research would back up this rejection of a pure spectator role in both the musical and the football experience. As was said at the beginning of this section the commercial institution offers services for money, but it also fails to limit rigidly what cannot be done by the buyer. This room for manoeuvre is the area that these boys are trying to control for themselves. Any visitor to football or dance halls over the past four years could not have failed to notice the attempts by those who run these institutions to limit that freedom to

---

*In fact the only serious football riot at Roker Park occurred after they had been beaten in their second successive home match by three clear goals. This was in the year after they were relegated, and a section of the crowd did in fact smash up part of the town after the match. Thus, obviously the extra-football activities are related to the football.

create their own non-spectator experience with the introduction of more bouncers, more stewards and, of course, more police.

The participation of these boys in the experience of a football match is a group experience with their mates. It represents a challenge to the mere spectator role of the sport and represents a possibility of the group *creation* of action. The action created – chanting, fighting, singing on the terraces, fighting, having a laugh in the dance hall – is action that represents the cultural background of the boys. There is none of the quiet appreciation of the skills of football or music that might characterise a more intellectually-inspired audience. Instead there is involvement and creation of their own kind of action. With regard to pop music this would also cut across the simplistic generational boundary drawn by the concept of 'teenage culture', since the experience of going to a dance hall would be different if one's own concern was the perception of the music, or the feeling of the physical dance. If it's the fights and the lasses that are important, then the structure of the music cannot be the main reason for going. Similarly with football. This represents a distinctive attitude to the total experience of these spare-time activities; a way of understanding them that does not see them as a means to an end, but rather as a *total experience*.

What role, then, do commercial institutions play in spare-time activity? The young people of the working class cannot command the resources and power to build their own institutions (in terms of bricks and mortar). This can be contrasted with the student union facilities at universities which can provide an alternative to the commercial institutions of the capitalist society around the university. Consequently the working-class boys must use these organisations, all of which are run primarily for profit. Nevertheless, the question of who controls these facilities is vital for them; it is important to try to understand that control, and their reaction to it.

These differences in the type of control experienced by the boys are directly related to the type of aims that the institutions have, and to what they are trying to do 'with' or 'for' the boy. The difficulties of, say, the youth clubs are immense in that they are attempting to change the boys' attitudes and behaviour, yet do not have the compulsory powers of attendance that the schools have.

Yet this differs from the nature of the control exercised by commercial institutions. The *aims* of commercial institutions are, primarily, to make money. As far as the boys are concerned, for a certain amount of money you can buy a certain amount of freedom, since the aim of the institutions is not primarily to interfere with the behaviour or ideas of those that enter them.

Thus if we were to compare the formal control structure of a dance hall and a youth club, it would be found that both are dominated and run by non-working-class adults. Nevertheless, if you were to look specifically at the way in which the organisation attempts to interfere with boys' behaviour, it is easy to see the way in which boys experience a greater amount of freedom in the dance halls. While they are limited within the dance hall, no one is trying to get them to *think* about something that they don't feel like; they can come as often or as seldom as they like. Both sides of the *commercial* contract respect the autonomy of the other, with the single and vital proviso of all capitalist institutions that the seller can refuse the buyer if he has not got the cash to fulfil the relationship.

The increasing economic power of the young has provided individual boys with some economic power, and this enables them to gain access to these institutions. The extent of this economic power in the hands of these particular boys who have not yet left school can be grossly overestimated, since they exist for the most part on pocket-money and part-time earnings. For these boys, dance halls are expensive places, and do not necessarily enter the realm of possible realistic choices on a Saturday evening. For *those* boys the street corner is the most likely institution open: it is cheap and always accessible. Consideration of the street will figure in most of the next group of activities dealt with in the next chapter.

The nature of both of the major institutions used by boys – the dance hall and the football ground – is changing. In the very recent past these institutions have tightened up on the amount of freedom that they allow their customers. Anyone who stands behind a goal at football matches at a first division club will realise that the increase in police activity in recent years has been enormous. Football programmes and statements in the local and national press show the clubs' dislike of the bad publicity given to them by the 'small minority of fans' that have been labelled soccer hooligans. This fear of 'public' reaction has led to a tightening up in social control in football grounds culminating, at the time of writing at any rate, in a member of the Football Association calling for the banning of all under 18-year-olds from football grounds. In dance halls recent years have seen the closing down of a number of smaller halls and the tightening of control within the two major chains, Rank and Mecca, which now try and exclude 'unruly' elements. In both institutions the amount of freedom open to the boys has been limited. This has increased the general importance of the street as an institution for youth spare-time activity.

Nevertheless, in terms of the boys' actual experience there is still an important difference between commercial and evangelical institutions.

Watching football: the T. V. and the ground

I've written about the boys' experience of going to a football match and tried to put it in the context of an experience outside a purely football-orientated one. Yet football itself does exist as a category of leisure activity. It must be understood, though, that most football is watched on the T. V., and in reporting these activities the timing of the research as pre-Sunderland-football-revival is obviously important. During the research Sunderland were relegated and football appeared to be in a sad state on Wearside. Briefly, during the revival, I would have expected to see much more activity based upon Sunderland as a team; such revivals are short-term-based, though, unless they represent a long-term change in the fortunes of the local club, as has happened at Leeds over the last twelve years. For the most part, though, T. V. plays the most important part in football-watching.

Question   Do you watch much football?
John S.   Every chance I can.
Question   Do you ever go to Roker Park?
John S.   Sometimes . . . not very often.
Question   Do you and your friends talk much about football?
John S.   Aye, when we come out on Sunday morning, we start to talk about *Match of the Day* from Saturday night.

Thus watching football is not necessarily a cold Saturday afternoon on the terraces. An interest in watching football *for the game in itself* as a spectator sport is in fact better served by watching the television than by watching Sunderland at Roker Park.

Question   Do you watch much football?
Edward   Saturday and Sunday on the telly. In the week when it's on.
Question   Do you go down Roker Park?

Edward Not much this year. It's not much, you know. When you see footy on the telly Roker Park isn't as good.
Question Why?
Edward Well, Leeds are just a lot better to watch than Sunderland.

Anyone who has watched football over the last couple of years will recognise that football as a game in terms of skill is indeed better to watch on telly, unless you live near a good first division side. Watching Liverpool, Leeds and Manchester United on the television every week had reduced the attraction of watching 'workmanlike' sides. Also, if you are purely interested in the skills of the game, the technology of television with its famous action replays shows the game much better.

Thus the question 'Are you interested in football?' was answered yes by 81 and no by ten. Yet an interest in football was never sufficient of itself to get people on to the terraces. There was another question, answered at a time when there had been nine or ten first-class games played at Roker that season; so six or more visits shows a fairly heavy commitment out of the possible opportunities:

How many times	Never	32
have you been	Once or twice	16
to Roker Park	Three to five times	13
this season?	Six or more	22
	No answer	10

Therefore, out of 81 very interested in soccer a large number seem never to go to Roker Park to watch football. I believe this backs up the impression about the different sorts of interest in the game that different sorts of supporters represent. 'Going to a football match' shows one sort of interest; watching footy on *Match of the Day* a very different sort. Therefore it becomes important, in trying to understand these activities, to look specifically at the structure of the activity as much as at the content.

Why, then, do boys get into trouble?

We are left, therefore, with a very different way of understanding 'getting into trouble' at football matches. The whole experience for the boys is a lot less instrumental than I at first thought: the getting into fights and so forth is also intelligible only in a different way. We must see it in relation to the *structured* leisure activities that are imposed upon the boys at youth clubs and schools. Within *these* structures activities occur for instrumental reasons. The boys reject those structures, and those organisations; when they take part in activities that they choose they create very different sorts of structures which allow them much greater possibilities of involvement. Once more, as in the educational system, it is of no use offering these boys involvement in the *content* of the activity; of itself this is rejected as a sham participation. It is essential for the boys to be allowed to create their own *structure* of activity. This is true in the fields of playing and watching sport, as well as music.

Footy and pop provide for these boys degrees of freedom from interference as a participator and a spectator. It provides them with an identity separate from those groups that are trying to mould their behaviour into more acceptable forms. Consequently, the Fulwell End at Roker Park, and all the equivalents all over the country, are playing a vital role in the maintenance of the boys' counter-culture at school and on the streets. What goes on in those 'ends' is intelligible to and experienced by only those involved. Teachers and policemen go along to watch football; but their interest and involvement are totally different. For the young supporter it represents a much more separate experience which he *knows* is only his own. He *knows* that a crowd of teachers chanting 'We hate Nottingham Forest . . .' is just not on. He also knows that he enjoys taking part in that. Therefore it reinforces the separate world of working-class youth; a separateness which becomes of political importance every Monday morning in the classroom. Without experiences such as these the boys would be much 'easier' for the teachers. If they did all take part in purely structured leisure activities, they would be able to accept the structures of work at school much more easily. The battles in the classrooms are therefore made fiercer by the 'aggro' on the terraces.

Similarly with pop music. Teenage working-class boys experience it very differently from their teachers. A visit to a Slade concert, where thousands of kids treat the auditorium much as they treat the rough end at the football match, shows the difference between the way they experience pop music and the way that their teachers do. Everyone at most concerts sings along with the music, has an involvement beyond the comprehension of anyone outside the culture. I've been to a Slade concert and learnt a lot about enjoying pop music, but I was there as an outsider looking in. These experiences, like football, provide 15-year-old working-class youth with a background which they play a part in creating. Pop music, even on the radio, is listened to in an entirely different way; lyrics and music are not separated out and dissected; different sorts of music are used for different sorts of 'background'. All of these experiences provide the boy at school with a culture that he can draw on in the conflict and, as such, both pop and footy are of political significance far beyond the simplistic way in which we usually view the politics of pop.

6
Why do kids get into trouble on the street?

The last chapter leaves us with an impression that kids enjoyed a certain sort of institution more than others because they could buy a certain amount of freedom in the dance hall, the disco and the football ground. This is true, but needs to be seen against the background of the institution that remains more strongly that of the boys – the street. All other activities in their spare time take place in relationship to the vast amount of time spent hanging about on the street. The difficult thing for all of us 'outsiders' to appreciate is that such activity is, in fact, *activity*, that it forms a series of actions which all of us feel are of no consequence. Indeed, one of the paradoxes of my research was my discovery that the main activity that the kids took part in was 'doing nothing', a phrase I had to learn to retranslate from its commonsense meaning. Within our own lives, leisure revolves around concrete action; we must realise that for these boys action has to be understood in entirely different ways.

The streets on a Saturday night and in the week have always provided the main arena for the leisure activities of working-class kids. It has been the arena where most of the illegal activities with juveniles happen. It is on the streets where the vast majority of vandalism takes place, where the greatest amount of fighting and thieving takes place. Therefore, since I was interested not only in juvenile delinquency but also in the boys' day-to-day part-time activities, the street was to be one of the major focuses of my interest in the kids. Street activity by youth has not been studied much by sociologists in this country, though this omission has been rectified by some recent studies. [1] The most famous studies of street life are those which have been carried out in the United States by a group of sociologists called the Chicago School. Members of this group have had an important effect upon the way in which all sociologists study young people and deviancy. They believed that it was important to study social phenomena on their own terms and consequently they pioneered the research method of participant observation. Most of the research into gangs of working-class youth has been carried out by means of participant observation. As I said in Chapter 1, this is not possible for a large Londoner in Sunderland working with 14-year-olds. What was possible, though, was to use their ideas if not their methodology.

They believed that it was only possible to understand phenomena such as juvenile misdemeanours in the context of the whole culture within which they took place. Thus the analysis of crime in Chicago in the inter-war period was carried out within an understanding of the immigrant culture of the Italians. Similarly, if I was to come to grips with juvenile vandalism and rule-breaking in general in Sunderland, it was necessary to put it in the context of the spare-time activities that the boys took part in. Therefore this chapter looks at kids getting into trouble on the streets as part of their Saturday evening activity; yet it does revolve around their getting into trouble. Therefore, I had to have some preconceptions about why kids got into trouble with the law; about why they broke society's rules. Recently a great deal of sociological endeavour has been spent theorising about why people break rules. The 1960s saw the creation of a whole 'industry' in the social sciences – the deviancy industry. For several years most of sociology spent its time analysing specific forms of rule-breaking in all different sorts of fields from drug-taking through youthful violence to a whole range of illegal activities. It seemed at one stage that no-one could break a rule anywhere without a sociologist coming along and trying to find out why. My research was part of this industry and as such I went into the project with a set of preconceptions about why kids broke rules.

Rule-breaking was seen as a *deliberate* activity. For too long sociologists in the past had said that individuals who broke rules did so for a whole range of unconscious or semi-conscious motives. The new deviancy theory gave the rule-breaker, the deviant, a consciousness about his or her actions; it presupposed that the deviant had some direction in his actions, and consequently a *knowledge* of the rules that he was breaking. Thus rule-breaking activity was aimed directly at the breaking of that particular rule. People broke rules for reasons.

Within the field of juvenile delinquency I expected to find a close relationship between kids breaking the law, smashing things and a deliberate rebelliousness. Those kids who were delinquent would be those who, perceiving what they were doing, would break the laws and telephone boxes with a certain deliberation. The background to this deliberation I had expected to find in the frustrations that emerged from their experiences of school. Thus I had expected to find a sort of anger at their powerless position at school being taken out on the community at large every Saturday night.

The actual situation was even further from my original misconceptions than the school situation. Saturday evenings were spent, for a whole variety of reasons, on the street. Once on the street the boys seemed to engage in a series of activities which they labelled as 'doing nothing'. Whilst 'doing nothing' some of them would have 'weird ideas'; and on many occasions a 'weird idea' would 'get them into trouble. Therefore I have entitled this section

How 'doing nothing' when added to a 'weird idea' equals 'getting into trouble'

The great majority of all the boys' spare-time activity was spent on the street, and before discussing the actual meaning of the activities on the street it is important to stress why the alternative institutions are not open to the boys as *real choices*.

Why not the youth club?

The youth club, being an evangelical institution, has all the limitations of those institutions as far as the boys are concerned. In the case of the youth club these limitations are of an obvious nature, and reside in the nature of the contradiction of the ideologies of the youth service — that is, between the need to reach youth and the need to change their behaviour in some way. Because of this contradiction, there is an appearance of freedom from the club that is soon denied. This contradiction was reflected in the boys' attitudes to youth clubs. While 35 out of 48 boys said that they liked going to a youth club only five admitted to actually going to a youth club on a Saturday evening. Of these only two actually mentioned the youth club as an 'organisation' they found attractive. Therefore for most of the boys 'going to a youth club' was an activity that did not include attendance and compliance with the organisation. Rather it is a place that exists physically as a building that provides shelter, and institutionally it plays a dual role: firstly, its official role, a place to play badminton;

secondly, as an institution that physically exists near the doorway of the club run by the authorities.

Question   What do you do on an average Saturday evening?
Charlie   Well, I go down the club to meet my mates.
Question   What do you do there?
Charlie   Just meet my mates and hang around. We don't go inside much.

Thus the institution of the youth club is transformed into the institution of the youth club's doorway. This latter institution is used by the boys for completely different purposes from those that the authorities might wish.

Why not commercial institutions?

As has been said above it is necessary to have sufficient economic power to gain entry into these organisations. For most of the boys most of the time, there is simply not enough cash.

Why not the house?

The only alternative left for these boys to the street is the house. The restrictions imposed upon groups of boys in the houses of their parents and the parents of their friends are less obvious and less articulated than those of the youth clubs.

However, a large number of boys do go and visit each other's homes on a Saturday evening and at other times, though the way that they do so betrays the limitations that are felt by the boys. Most of them talked of going down to their mate's home and staying there for a while before coming out again. Three examples of this:

Question   What do you do on an average Saturday evening?
Mac   Well, it's like this: I go out with me friends, we walk about, we might go in one of the houses and then we come back in and watch football on telly.
Question   What do you do on an average Saturday evening?
John S.   I just go down me friend's house and we all stop in there for a bit and watch television, and we just go out and call for some other mates, go down to the shop and buy some chips and come back and watch telly.

Question What do you do on an average Saturday evening?
Doug Go round me mate's house, and watch telly, if his mum and
dad aren't in, then get together, and go out and hang around.

Homes, as far as Saturday evening spare-time activities are
concerned, are essentially places where parents are either absent or
present, and also where the television is. If the parents are present,
then this severely restricts the amount of freedom available to the
boys. Saturday probably represents the only evening when the boys
can get together to watch the telly in the parents' absence, so this does
present a real attraction for the boys. Also *Match of the Day* is on the
box and it can be watched with your mates in a simulated crowd
activity, as against watching *Shoot* with your dad on a Sunday
afternoon.

If the television is the attraction for the boys, what then are the
detractions? These are never articulated by the boys, but judging by
the constant movement out of the house (not one boy said that he
went round to his mate's and stayed there all evening) they do NOT
feel at ease as a group in each other's houses. The interaction of a
Saturday night out requires a high degree of freedom to create and
follow the 'weird ideas' that occur to the boys. In their parents' homes
the possibilities of coming into contact with the forces of social
control are almost inescapable. If something goes wrong there is no
chance of running away, or of not being identified, and whilst Klein[2]
and others see parental control in working-class homes as 'weak and
inconsistent' she has not had to face a father who has just discovered
on Sunday morning that the telly was broken by his son's friends the
night before. Such authority represents a constant check upon
behaviour, a check that leaves even less room for manoeuvre than the
youth club.

In this way, having been priced out of the cinema, dance halls and
having walked out of the clubs and homes, the boys are left with
nothing but the street. But on mentioning the negative aspects of the
other possibilities of places to go on a Saturday night, I want also to
outline the positive aspects of the street. The boys are not simply
driven out by elimination of choices on to the streets; there is also an
element of positive choice about the street as a venue for action. It *is*
free in both commercial terms and in terms of close control. The
possibility of a range of different actions is great in the street. Most
importantly it is in the street where the boys can decide what they

want to do, when they want to do it, and when they want to stop it, more than any other place.

Question   What do you do on an average Saturday evening?
Frank   On Saturday I usually go about with my friends and that, knock about and have a few laughs.
Question   Have a few laughs?
Frank   Well, we just go anywhere that we want really; there's no certain limit to where we go, really; we just don't bother to make any arrangements. We just tell jokes and what we've done during the day.

Question   Do you ever just knock about the streets with your mates?
Roland   Yes, a lot. Just about in the streets deciding what to do with the time.

So, whilst it is true, as one boy said, that 'we stand on the corner because there is nowhere else to stand', the street does give a great deal of freedom to boys who feel they are closely watched at school. It allows the group to have autonomy over its action, to have its 'weird ideas' and to carry them out.

It is important to mention the importance within the context of the use of the streets of the boys' overriding passion – namely, playing and talking about footy. (This is no place for a discourse on why playing football has such fantastically strong support as a day-to-day activity among working-class youth; here I will try to make sense of the meaning of the game for these boys.) I have already discussed the importance of the structure of the actual playing of the game as far as the boys are concerned (that is, most of the boys saw a distinct difference between playing football in an organised team every Saturday or Sunday, and kicking a ball around when and where they felt like it). What is immediately important in discussing the choice of location of this activity is why the street is chosen. Obviously, if boys want to play football then they need a wide and preferably flat area to play in. There are few such areas in working-class estates. The one open space in Municipal estate was in the centre near the school, and it was hopelessly bumpy to play footy on. As far as the boys were concerned the street and its immediate environs were the only places to engage in their favourite activity.

Thus effectively the boys were left with only the streets to go to on a Saturday evening, after an hour or two of watching telly. Yet also the street provided them with room and freedom resulting from lack of control to decide exactly what they wanted to do. Importantly, too, it provided an area for them to play football.

Why in groups?

All previous research into rule-breaking and non-rule-breaking activity of working-class youth in their spare time has noted that all activities are carried out in groups. The immediate response in every interview, except one, to the question 'What do you do on an average Saturday night?' was to mention repeatedly the 'mates' of the boys being interviewed. Thus very obviously, the boys experience all spare-time activity as group activity (which is of course the same way that they experience school). Street activity particularly was always in a group. It is not possible to explicate the social psychological background of the group experience fully, nor is it possible to discuss historically the group nature of working-class experience over time. Both of these would be necessary to answer fully the question 'Why in groups?', and there is insufficient space. However, I would argue that the way to 'individualist action' and 'self-fulfilment' is never there for the boys of Sunderland. J. B. Mays comments upon this lack in Liverpool youth in a derogatory tone, by seeing it as a 'lack of individual resourcefulness and a failure to achieve the methods of expressing oneself'.[3] Using an analysis that was based upon the appreciation of cultural diversity, it is possible to perceive this group action as being part of a cultural background of working-class behaviour rather than a pathological 'lack' of any supposedly universalistic behaviour. Thus the boys that referred to their mates constantly when talking of Saturday night were referring to the group nature of the solution to something that was experienced by them *as a group problem*. Certain of their problems were experienced as collective and these allowed for the collective working out of solutions. Many writers discuss this in their work: within the sub-cultural tradition Cohen[4] and Downes;[5] within the political tradition Lenin[6] and Mao.[7] All these writers point towards the way in which certain problems can only be met collectively rather than individually. I would suggest that Saturday night in Sunderland is one such problem.

Why do 'nothing'?

Having established the importance of both the street and the group in

these boys' activities it is vital now to try to understand why the main
activity of the boys was 'doing nothing'. This is undoubtedly the most
difficult question to answer as it contains a whole series of problems
that, at first, appear to be simply semantic; but in many ways this is
the crux of the problem. As has been commented the previous studies
seem to have missed this point in attempting to understand the spare-
time activities of working-class youth. Yet in focusing our attention
upon the activity of 'doing nothing' or 'just knocking about' we
immediately see that, experientially for the boys and analytically for
us, this is in fact doing something. This is despite the fact that the boys
themselves describe it as doing nothing.

Question   What sort of things do you do on an average Saturday?
Derek   Just go round to a house, watch telly, play a few records, just
walk around.
Question   Walk around?
Derek   There's not much to do.
Question   What?
Derek   Just walk around.

Question   What sort of things do you do with your mates in the
streets?
Adam   Stand around . . . nothing really.
Question   What do you do?
Adam   We don't do anything much.
Question   Nothing at all?
Adam   No, just stand around.

These seemingly repetitious interviews were carried out many
times on different boys. As far as most of them were concerned, when
they tried to explain they did seem to do nothing on a Saturday
evening. Yet are they in fact doing nothing when they are 'doing
nothing'? I have already outlined the existence of something –
namely, standing on corners in groups. However, as far as these boys
are concerned nothing memorable seems to happen to them on a
Saturday night. It is important to repeat briefly the methodological
point here about language – that in asking these boys these questions,
we are in fact imposing alien techniques of thinking and reasoning.
The boys continue to give a seemingly endless series of dead-pan
answers to the questions because the questions assume that there is
something *more* going on; that standing around is a means to an end.

Whereas in terms of their own experience standing around on street corners is done in order to . . . stand around on street corners; the experience itself justifies the experience; they don't gather on street corners in order to plan rule-breaking acts; they don't walk around the streets in order to *do* anything. Thus when I repeatedly ask 'What *were* you doing?', the boy repeatedly answers what they were in fact doing – nothing.

Doing nothing, then, does not deserve to be neglected as an activity simply because the boys do not articulate the sort of activities it contains. For the main part a great deal of talking seems to go on when 'nothing' is being done.

Question What sort of things do you do when you are just walking about?

John S. Just talk.

Question Talk?

John S. Just talk.

Question Does anything ever happen to you?

John S. Nothing much. We keep moving about all the time so someone can't complain.

Question Complain?

John S. Well, people complain and we get into trouble. Not for doing owt but for just standing about.

Question What sort of thing do you do with your mates?

Duncan Just stand around talking about footy, about things.

Question Do you do anything else?

Duncan Joke, lark about, carry on. Just what we feel like really.

Question What's that?

Duncan Just doing things. Last Saturday someone started throwing bottles and we all got in.

Question What happened?

Duncan Nothing really.

Standing around talking among themselves seems to have a real importance to the boys which mirrors the importance of talking in school and the importance of silence to the teacher. This also responds closely to Whyte's *Street Corner Society*,[8] where the street corner represented the only chance of the men to get together and talk things over on their own. This can be undervalued by observers who feel free *at any time* to assert their ideas in almost any circumstance.

Talking, as is the case with most of these experiences, cannot be simply fitted into a simplistic means—end scheme – that is, the boys do *not* talk in order to explicate their ideas or to search for some kind of truth. Rather they stand around and exchange stories which need never be true or real, but which are as interesting as possible. About football, about each other; talking not to communicate ideas but to communicate the experience of talking. It passes the time and it underlines the group nature of this method of passing the time. Not only football and pop music were talked about; and a great deal of joking goes on. It was between the area of talking, joking and carrying on that things emerged that the boys called 'ideas'. These 'ideas' formed the basis for group action and it is the way in which these spontaneously evolve and are carried out that constitutes one of the most active elements of 'hanging about'. (Incidentally it is interesting that school never seems to be talked about much for very long after school hours. Observations at the end of the school day showed that the major topic of conversation whilst waiting at the bus stop was what happened at school, but by the time the boys got off the bus school did not impinge significantly upon their discussions unless something really important had happened.)

'Weird ideas'

Question   Do you ever go out and knock about with the lads?
Albert   Sometimes, when I feel like it.
Question   What do you do?
Albert   Sometimes we get into mischief.
Question   Mischief?
Albert   Well, somebody gets a weird idea into their head, and they start to carry it out, and others join in.
Question   Weird idea?
Albert   Things . . . like going around smashing milk bottles.

Boys on a Saturday night in Sunderland, in a group, on a street corner, are aware that they are 'doing nothing' and are bored with it in their own minds, essentially wanting something to happen. They want to have an interesting or an exciting time, a time that would not be boring, where they could create some action. For the most part they seem fairly sure that this only rarely happens, but their Saturday night activity can best be understood as an attempt to maximise the chances that they will be involved in something remarkable (literally worthy of remark; see the above discussion of talking). Consequently we must not be surprised if they see their Saturday evenings spent on the streets as boring; rather we must compare it with their perceptions of being involved in something exciting. These perceptions are obviously linked with what they expect from certain pastimes – for example, they *know* that nothing exciting will happen at home with mum and dad; they perceive a small chance of something happening around a youth club, and a slightly larger chance of something happening on a street corner. So even if they are bored every Saturday evening there is *always* the chance that something will happen the following Saturday.

If we analyse the street corner activity of doing nothing in groups in the light of always hoping that something will happen, then the creation and the putting into effect of 'ideas' by the group can be seen as one of the most significant group experiences. Their significance is not only in terms of the group experience but also in terms of the wider society, for it is these ideas born out of the street corner groups, doing nothing, that are to a large extent the 'juvenile delinquency' of the police and criminologists. Most significantly, these ideas are born out of boredom and the expectation of future and continuing boredom, and this affects the sort of ideas that they are. A good 'idea' must contain the seeds of continuing change (from the boring situation) as well as excitement and involvement. Smashing milk bottles is a good example of this since it typifies the way in which they are put into effect. Methodologically, it is not possible for any researcher to get the kids to talk with much sense of ideas since the question 'Why?' to the smashing of milk bottles is one that is not possible for the boy to answer outside the context of the whole Saturday evening.

Question What sort of things do you do with your mates?
Mac Just knock about.
Question Doing what?
Mac Not much really; things just happen, like smashing milk bottles.
Question Why did you do that?
Mac I dunno . . . er . . .

Question What do you do on street corners?
Dick Police never saw us do anything wrong, so they shouldn't pick on us. But we just used to play around, smashing things.

Question　What sort of things?
Dick　Anything really.
Question　Why?
Dick　I dunno . . . just ideas.

The answer to the last question, for example, is not really possible within the boys' own terms, outside the total experience of the time. For the sort of interaction that we are referring to here is not the *planned* smashing of things. It is not that boys go out on a Saturday night looking for milk bottles or other things to smash. Rather they use smashing as something interesting to do.

Question　What do you do when you just knock around the streets?
Richard　Sometimes get into fights, or trouble, but mostly nothing much.
Question　Just try and give me an example.
Richard　Er . . . last Saturday we was hanging about and someone kicked a bottle over and it smashed. Then we all started smashing bottles.

Smashing things does seem to be an important component of these 'ideas'. Indeed this would appear to go to a wider set of objects apart from milk bottles since only 18 out of 93 boys had not smashed something like a streetlamp in the past year.

Question　What sort of things do you do on a Saturday evening?
Peter　Usually play football down the streets, play footy. Just gang down the Court or somewhere then come home.
Question　What other things do you do?
Peter　On Sunday I knock around with me mates.
Question　What do you do?
Peter　Well, cause trouble, you know; play knocking on doors, throw stones at windows and that. Cause fights mostly.

Is it *really* necessary to explain the excitement of smashing things, whether they are milk bottles, shop windows, buses, telephone boxes or whatever, if the alternative is to stand there and do nothing? Whilst it is true that there is no real premeditation to smash things up, it is in the genesis of such ideas that we would expect such concepts as deviance amplification to be of importance. A group of boys who are bored and are standing on a street corner are much more likely to have the idea of smashing up something that has been perceived as being smashed up before, not necessarily in any imitative sense, but mainly because it will be in their consciousness as something which can be smashed. This form of amplication is a fairly complex model that doesn't in fact need the name, since it differs from the original model. But, given the likely creation of ideas by the boys in street corners, these ideas are going to reflect the boys' consciousness. On each Saturday evening this will be affected by things that have occurred to them through local channels of communication or through the mass media.

The most notable single case was recounted to me one lunch-hour by three boys sitting on the 'green' in the middle of Municipal estate. They told me about their Saturday night activities of about a month ago. This group were just knocking about the streets and they walked past a closed youth club. They stood around the youth club for a while and then someone said that it would be better inside the club. So the group broke into the club and once inside said that they felt really great walking about in the dark – 'like spies' trying not to make a noise. Then someone started scrapping with another boy, the lights were put on and the scene was immediately transformed to a barroom brawl in the wild west with boys being knocked over tables, smashing up chairs and mirrors. Importantly the fight itself was not a 'real' one but the scenario being played out was. After some while when most of the furniture (including table-tennis table) was smashed up, 'the Sheriff came to the door just like in the films' – that is, the police. Then all the boys were scattered and some were caught by the police.

The boys claimed that hundreds of pounds' worth of damage was done. Could this damage have been seen as 'caused' by certain media scenarios, namely those of spy films and cowboys? This interpretation does not fit with the boys' account. Whilst it is true that they were playing out these scenarios in their own way, it could not be said that they had caused the scene itself.

Getting into fights

One of the most common diversions for the boys is getting into a fight. Again, within the context of 'doing nothing' on a street corner, fights are an important and exciting occasion. Interest in fights and the pulling power of fights as against other pastimes is best exemplified by the result of a single shout of 'fight' in a school playground. If we look at the interest in fights and fighting as an aspect apart from its background then we *do* need some form of explanation along the lines advanced by David Downes when he talks about the need to defend virility.[9] Also if we look at gang fights apart from their background then we also need some form of territory concept as an *explanation* of the fights.

However, if we once more try and understand these fights in terms of boys hanging around on street corners, then we can see that a fight is simply an easy and an interesting event, and that this in itself is sufficient for us to understand its importance for the boys. It is exciting and it is something that can be easily brought about. In the same way as the boys relate to football, fights represent a totally unstructured piece of action which is under the control of the boys and whose relationship with the 'fight game' is as distant as the relationship between footy and Wembley. So once more, rather than posit the cause of the action from purely within the fight, we must look at the context of the whole life experience.

But looking for a fight does seem to have two sets of meanings. For some of the boys concerned it was a casual occurrence that they were excited about when it happened. For others it was the major occurrence of every Saturday night, and they actively styled their 'doing nothing' as looking for a fight — some of this second group styled themselves skinheads.

Question What do you do on an average Saturday night?
Dave Saturday night, why . . . er . . . we usually go around an off-licence and get something to drink. Some cider or some beer. We usually go round me mate's place and play records, watch telly and then just knock about.
Question What do you do when you're knocking about?
Dave Just kick about, play football or something, cause a bit of mischief around the streets.
Question Mischief?
Dave Well, we just seem to get into it on the streets.
Question Do you get into any fights?
Dave No . . . well, not many.

Question What do you do when you hang about?
Ivan Not much, play a bit of footy, get into a fight perhaps.

With these two boys it is fruitless simply to try to explain why they fight, since the drive towards fighting is not a vitally important part of their lives that can be teased out from the whole context. Given nothing to do, something happens, even if it is a yawn, or someone sitting down on somebody else's foot, or someone turning over an old insult or an old injury, and it's this, in the context of 'nothing', that leads to fights — something diminutive and unimportant outside the context of 'doing nothing', yet raging and vital within that context. For others, though, fights have a slightly more important set of meanings. Saturday evening is *likely* to contain some fights for these boys.

Question   What do you do on an average Saturday evening?
Steven   Oh, I go down the town and knock around with the skins . . . the skinheads.
Question   What do you do?
Steven   Go in the Wimpy, or jump on some boys or something . . . kick them.
Question   Do you ever get into trouble for kicking boys?
Steven   If we are knocking about in gangs. The police pick on us for just knocking about in gangs. I've been down the police station twice for just knocking about in gangs.
Question   What sort of things do you do with the lads?
Steven   Well, you know the Grand Prix down there, well, we duff the machines up and get free goes on them. You know the Corporation buses — when they go in for a cup of tea we all go and open the doors and kick the buses in.
Question   Do you play footy with the lads?
Steven   Sometimes . . . we have scraps, you know, kicking them in.

Question   What do you do on an average Saturday evening?
Fred   I go down the station, you know, in the town centre, and shoot through to Newcky, a whole gang of us, then we walk around Newcky, ready for trouble. We find a few Maggie supporters and kick them in, have a good scrap we do.
Question   What do the police do?
Fred   They try and stop us sometimes, catch us, but I give a false name and address because they think I'm from Newcky.
Question   What sort of fights?
Fred   Well, not real fights, as some of them might be quite matey. But still, when you put the boot in, you put the boot in, but we are friendly after, like.

Question   What do you do on an average Saturday evening?
Paul   I knock around in a gang and we get into fights, scraps, you know.
Question   What sort of fights?
Paul   Well, we meet up with another gang and start chucking milk bottles at them mainly the South Sipton gang.
Question   Why do you do that?
Paul   So they can't get near us.
Question   What happens when they do?
Paul   We have a scrap; it's good fun.
Question   Do people get hurt?
Paul   No.

For these boys the 'excitement of the fight' has become institutionalised. It is not *spontaneously* undertaken against a backdrop of boredom from which it emerges as a highlight; rather it becomes a form of activity that is organised in order to remove the boredom that created it. In fighting, as with football, those boys that particularly enjoy an activity and are good at it will spend more time ensuring that they are engaged in that activity. They will create institutions where this is possible. The way the boys talk about them it is fairly obvious that the fights between, say, Newcastle and Sunderland supporters are only incidentally about football and more about the mode and structure of the activity of fighting compared to its perceived alternatives. You bash up the 'Maggie supporters' not because Newcastle play a better game of football but because the alternatives are not at all exciting. This explains the way in which the fights are 'real' and 'not real' at the same time. They *must* be convincing to create sufficient feeling as an activity, for if the boys know its a con then they also know they are not fighting. At the same time 'you are still mates' even though the boot is really put in. In a 'real' fight the boys know that they really get hurt, but 'real fights' depend upon 'real grievances' that might occur when Sunderland are beaten 4–0 by Newcastle. This, however, does not happen every Saturday, so the boys manufacture sufficient disagreement to create fights and excitement. One could hypothesise that the Municipal gang throw milk bottles at the South Sipton gang because they are defending their 'territory'. If the boys are given a chance to talk about fights in the context of 'Saturday's bother', it remains archetypally an activity, an activity created in the knowledge that the alternative is, very likely, nothing.

With football, the content of the 'gang warfare' is not unimportant but can lead us to misunderstand the situation. The content of the fighting comes from a much deeper cultural involvement, the important concerns of working-class culture, such as 'the fucking Fenians' in the Shankill, the bloody troops in the Bogside and the apparently perverse ascendancy of Newcastle United Football Club in Sunderland. No boy can possibly grow up ignorant of these vitally important areas of life. A fine example of the content of fights is a full-scale riot that happened to take place in the precincts of Municipal School during the period of the research but was unfortunately not observed by the researcher. The basketball team of Municipal School went to play at Tavistock School, inflicting several injuries upon the opposing team. The Municipal basketball team was manned by players who believed that you should 'play basketball dirty'. After the game, the whole of the fourth year of Tavistock School roughed up the Municipal basketball team as a reprisal for the injuries. The next week the Tavistock basketball team had to come to Municipal School to play the return fixture. Word had gone round about the previous battle and after the game (a similar rough-house won by Municipal) the whole of the fourth year of Municipal was waiting around the school gates to repeat the beating handed out by Tavistock School the week before. However, what one boy (Billy) described as the 'whole fucking school' turned up from Tavistock to defend their team. A full-scale bundle ensued. It would be ridiculous to posit this fight as 'hooligans driven by loyalty to the school basketball team' (basketball hooligans) yet this WAS the context of the fight. The school had provided the issue (loyalty) and the easy differentiation of the two sides (uniform) but this could never be seen as the cause.

Any fight, then, whether between two boys, two gangs or hundreds of people has a meaning and importance that is only intelligible within the alternatives available to the boys. The content of the fights tends to reflect, for the most part, traditional concerns of the cultures that the boys grew up in, rather than anything that they created. This would explain the ambivalence of the working-class community as a whole to the content of fights in working-class youth. In football, the gangs of skinheads ARE good supporters, but are still hooligans.

Getting into trouble

As was suggested above, the boys' experience of spare time does involve contact at some time with the police. Most of the quotes from the boys have already mentioned getting into trouble. My discussion of street corner activity has attempted to show the important factor of the street; it also shows how the street provides, if anywhere does, a 'natural' area for group activity. Therefore given the police attitude to the street (that is, historically the police are there to keep the streets safe) and that the boys see the street as the natural arena for their activity then there will *inevitably* be interaction between these two discrete groups. The meaning of the interaction for the boy is vital to any understanding of how boys get into trouble.

It is possible to hypothesise that the reason that the boys get into trouble is that trouble provides excitement; that they are aware of the 'ban' on street activity that is created by the police ideology of order in the street and that it is this awareness of 'ban' that creates the impetus for street activity. In the boys' terms, 'getting into trouble' is the reason for 'knocking about on the street'. The hypothesis that I would put forward to account for getting into trouble of this kind is different in emphasis. It posits an experiential naïvety on the part of the boys with regard to the police *ideology* of order on the street. The boys are on the street for all the reasons outlined above – summed up by the phrase 'we stand on the corners because there is nowhere else to stand'. In other words, the street is the culturally-perceived place to spend spare time irrespective of police activity. Indeed, as I have shown, it is perceived as being one of the places freest of social control, and allowing the greatest amount of freedom. It is, however, precisely these activities that are most noticeable for the police as being possible infringements of order. I am not saying that the boys take part in a range of activities and that the police clobber them for some of them; rather they spend most time on the street, just 'knocking about', and it is precisely THAT activity that is disliked by the police. For as we have seen knocking about *does* consist of activities that are nearly all rule-breaking: playing footy in the street, fighting, smashing things, getting 'weird ideas'; though they are not activities entered into *because* they are rule-breaking but because they provide diversification and excitement. It is only on introducing another powerful group, the police, that the *idea* of ban enters and then as an institution that implements this idea through *power* rather than through a set of common values.

It is only this basic naïvety about the work of the police that would account for the persistence in both the activity AND the surprise at the intervention of the police. The surprise and indignation is not a feigned expression but pervades nearly every mention of police activity with regard to these boys. There seems to be no feeling of 'legitimisation' given to the police interference in the boys' actions, no feeling of a 'fair cop'. This reflects very strongly the model of control in the school, where there was no real recognition of the moral or legal rights of the teacher to interfere. Similarly with the police, the only way in which their rights of interference are recognised is through their *power* and that is recognised, like the teacher, *only* in physical presence.

This puts a different gloss upon Matza's 'Techniques of Neutralisation'.[10] For, while he is right in saying that the activities are not committed as acts of rebellion or ideological commitment to wrong, neither are they committed *despite* the banning of them. The events spoken about by these boys are intelligible only through a very real indignation that the activity is banned by police power. Matza's boy saying that lots of people do it is not necessarily apologetic; rather he is simply stating the obvious as he sees it. For our boys, there is no common rationality that says what would happen if we all smashed telephone boxes or milk bottles, because nearly everybody does. It is not that they are ideologically committed to street corners, to playing footy or to smashing things; rather these are the things that they do; they do them against a backdrop of doing nothing. Then the police come along and move you on. The concept of ban does not occur in this situation.

The power of the police is seen as virtually total by the boys, and this perception is backed by studies of the police[11] which stress the arbitrary nature of the police power at this level of interaction. This, coupled with the complete lack of understanding of the workings of the court system,[12] means that it is correct to say that the power of the policeman is seen as total; he can hit you, put your name in the book or put you in probation or in approved school away from your home and mates. It is this power that gives police activity its importance for the boys rather than any common idea of ban. Activity on the streets is carried on with this *power* in mind, a power that does not let you play football, stand around, smash things or fight, though not necessarily with any glimpse of the law or of the set of ideas behind police activity. The police, like the teachers, are a group of people with power that do some very strange and arbitrary things; their power is massive and has to be coped with, if not obeyed. As in the classroom, the methods of coping with individuals with power are many and varied, like giving wrong names and addresses.

Whilst the boy *has* to go to school to cope with the teacher, there is a lot more choice contained in the creation of this situation and it is important to outline the boys' perceptions of how they get into situations of trouble.

Question   Do you ever knock around the streets?
Ian   Sometimes.
Question   What happens?
Ian   Sometimes we have a Panda around us for playing football or something like that.
Question   What?
Ian   Well, you know, just hanging around minding our own business.
Question   What happens then?
Ian   Well . . . er . . . (laughs) you've got to run.
Question   Do you like playing footy?
Ian   Well, you see, where we play football, like behind the shop, the people that live above the shop complained, then the Panda came round.

Question   What do you do on an average Saturday evening?
John S.   Saturday night we sometimes go out and play footy, like. Though it depends what's on the telly, but most Saturdays we just walk about.
Question   What sort of things do you do when you walk about?
John S.   Just talk.
Question   Does anything else happen?
John S.   Nothing much. We keep moving about all the time so someone can't complain.
Question   Complain?
John S.   Well, people complain and we get into trouble. Not for doing owt but for just standing about.

Question   What do you do when you hang around?
Martin   I spend most of me time in me mate's home. Sometimes we go fishing. On the streets we just stand around in groups, doing lots of things on your own, but you can get into trouble there.
Question   Trouble?
Martin   Yes, the police don't like you just hanging about.

Question   Do you ever just knock about the streets?
Jimmy   Yes, that's what we do every day.

Question Do you ever get into trouble?
Jimmy Yes, I was getting into trouble for playing inside a club, I was getting picked up by the police. It's just because we were on the premises and they caught us.
Question What else?
Jimmy Sometimes when you're fighting you get caught by the coppers.
Question How does trouble start?
Jimmy Well, we were just playing football, minding our own business, and police will come up and argue with you. Sometimes they'll hit you and sometimes they'll just take your name.

The boys see trouble as something connected purely with the police, or other social control agents; one cannot get into trouble without the presence of one of these groups. At no stage do they perceive it as *doing* wrong, or breaking rules. Indeed the question 'Why?', asked about getting into trouble, is a question to do only with the presence of the police rather than with any rules or morals. This must be linked with the naïve entry into 'trouble', for if indeed they do just walk around the streets, what rules are they breaking? What wrongs are they doing if they just walk around the streets and the police harass them? The reasons for the harassment lie with the police and NOT inside any rule that the boys are breaking, since for the boys the streets are a 'natural' meeting place. Indeed this perception of the boys does agree with another analysis based upon a historical interpretation about the role of the police as clearers of riff-raff off the street. The role of the police and the role of the education system are parallel here, because they are both attempting to change the styles of living of people who already exist and are seen as threatening by ruling groups within society. Whilst this may appear similar to Lemert's original formulation about primary deviation,[13] it does attempt to locate interaction ideas in a specific view of the state as an organisation attempting to attack and change styles and behaviour that are not *in themselves* deviant.
In general, this would argue for a shift away from what appears to be the motive force of deviance research – that is, the juvenile delinquent, the truant and the schizophrenic – to the initial motive force of the interaction, *as planned by the police and the law, the education system, and the psychiatrist.*
The boys' experience of the interaction between themselves and the police is of an attempt by the police to interfere, and this attempt is

interpreted only through the power of the police and the law, and not through any *belief* in the validity of the moral rules and laws that the police interpret. Thus there *were* boys who had left the groups in which had walked around the streets because they kept on getting into trouble.

Question What do you do on an average Saturday evening?
Dick At about one o'clock the rink starts, and I sometimes go. If I dinna go there, I go down the girl's house.
Question What do you do down the rink?
Dick I just sit down and walk around.
Question Do you ever knock around the streets with your mates?
Dick I used to, we used to, about three or four months ago. We used to go up the park gates and we used to carry on and that. The park-keeper used to come every night and chase us. Sometimes we used to stand on street corners and then the police would come and chase us.
Question Why?
Dick I dunno, but it got so they knew us and kept on picking on us.
Question What did you do on street corners?
Dick Police never saw us do anything wrong, so they shouldn't pick on us, but we just used to play about. Sometimes smashing things, you know.
Question What sort of things?
Dick Anything, really. I dunno why, just ideas people had.
Question Why did you stop knocking around?
Dick It got dangerous.

This interview manages to get across the whole story of the experience of getting into trouble for the boys. It does so by looking at the whole process over a time-span. Therefore we see that rules are not broken *specifically because they are rules*; rules are broken for the most part as a by-product of the flow of the activity engaged in by the boys. If the boys want to go around breaking rules, then that is easy enough. However, the major aspect of rules for these boys is the power of the enforcer rather than the existence of the rules in abstract, as a thing apart from the activity. As I found out from their experience of school, such a view of 'rules' as the latter is a very middle-class phenomenon. In order for us to understand the behaviour which we may, and the police certainly do see, as rule-breaking, we must see it experienced as part of a locus of experience (that is, knocking about in groups on street corners doing nothing) rather than as a piece of activity (a fight) staged to break rules. The action is the result of a cultural milieu; the rule which forbids it is the result of a powerful section of the community forbidding that action. Therefore the essence of the *rule-breaking* part of the activity is to be found in the group that has banned it, rather than in the group that carries it out.

Similarly, Dick stopped breaking the rules on the streets not because smashing things had become defined as wrong by him, but because the power of the police was recognised as being against that activity. It is important to note that he did not simply stop smashing things in the street, which is all the police *in law* could stop, but he stopped *all* activity in the street. This very sensibly recognises the police ideology; that is, against all youth activity in the streets; it recognises that any boys walking around the street in a group are breaking the rules, rather than only those who smash things. In these circumstances it is not possible to expect boys to have a clear perception of what rule-breaking activity is as compared with non-rule-breaking activity; for the police will harass you even if you are 'doing nothing' at all. Under these circumstances it is possible to say that most juvenile delinquency undertaken by these boys is, experientially, the result of certain parts of actions that *they* consider culturally unremarkable. However, these activities are forbidden by powerful groups that exist outside that cultural milieu. If we are interested in rule-breaking activity, therefore, we cannot simply pull out these activities so labelled by the outside world and say that they are either a causally valid or an experientially valid group of activities for the boys. For them, they go out on the streets, and are set on by 'the coppers', who stop them from taking part in certain activities. It is with the power of the police that the idea of infraction or rule-breaking emerges into the activity.

7
What you gonna do about it?

Youth, class and the state

The previous five chapters have all been relating the experiences of working-class youth to some of the ideas of sociology, most notably and consistently the idea that 'values' are the major constraint on their actions. This has been shown to be idealistic in both the experiences of education and of leisure and rule-breaking. Actions cannot simply be understood as a rejection of or an attack on 'middle-class values'; instead it is a consistent reaction to the use of power by teachers and by the state in the form of law. This perspective is not analytically explored in the book; it is not followed up by detailed theoretical and sociological understanding of the position of youth in society. It will be necessary to carry through an analysis of a whole book to make any coherent sense of these questions.

Yet it would be irresponsible to leave the discussion at this point, to fail to relate this to much wider debates and discussions. These conclusions, therefore, are not an attempt to 'point out areas for further research'; they will instead put the material contained in this book into the current political context of the debates and discussions about the position of youth in society, especially the educational debate opened by the Prime Minister in October 1976.

The politics of research findings

It is always tempting for practitioners to turn to the last chapter of a book on, for example, teaching or social work, and look for the direct implications for their practice. Nine times out of ten these are then dismissed as 'too simplistic' or 'out of touch'; this is inevitably the case whenever overt prescriptions for practice are put forward by social scientists not facing the actual experience of practice. This leaves us not putting forward practice prescriptions, which in turn means that practitioners will tend to attack the work as 'purely theoretical' or 'no use on Monday morning'.

Given the stance that the sociological profession has taken up within the political struggle in this country this is hardly surprising. Sociologists have continually pretended that it can come up with the goods necessary to change this or that problem. It has disappointed because it remains a part of an intellectual workforce that is in some sense apart from the society that it is investigating. As a consequence it has never had the real contacts with social and political forces to give any weight to the elements of change that are contained in its work. It has investigated, published and, to a large extent, sat back waiting; nothing has happened so it has started another investigation. Such intellectual work will, in so far as it comes up with answers at all, come up with simplistic intellectual answers because it will not be taking as its problems those problems experienced by sections of the world around it. In so far as we construct our problems *apart* from society, then our conclusions are located outside the political processes of change in that society.

It is imperative that sociologists not only relate their findings to the political world around them, but also try and take their problems from the day-to-day political world. In the past this has simply been seen by social scientists as relating their problems to those in power in the state; here we have moved against this to create our own view of problems. Yet, since these views are isolated from the mainstream of political life, it becomes necessary for us to develop ways of studying problems of subordinate groups or indeed, finally, working-class problems.

In this book I have ONLY moved towards this position. I did not create the initial problematic of the work in close consultation with the boys; I did not get an overall *class* view of the problems of education from working people. Yet there is movement in this direction and it is important at this stage of the book to try and relate the ideas that have sprung from it to the problems that working-class people face in the educational context. I will also try and relate it concretely to teachers' experience and work.

Progressive education and 'educational turmoil'

One question that this book must face up to is whether there has been an increase in disorder in schools; and whether this increase has been caused by a relaxation of discipline.

Of course one study at one time cannot conclusively answer such a question, but to fail to relate my findings to such an important question would be a gross cop-out.

What are the various positions on this debate?

The new authoritarians

Firstly there is the body of opinion that sees the changes that have taken place in schools as having been a major cause in the rise of school disorder. The arguments connect the 'progressive' movements in education with a naïve belief in young people's capacity to make their own decisions about a whole range of issues both inside and outside schools. Such a belief is thought to be naïve because most people, and especially children, cannot cope with a wide range of choices and as such they really need strong intellectual and moral direction. Such arguments are linked to the notion that the moral fibre of society is collapsing, undermined by permissiveness in a number of arenas, but with schools being of paramount importance in having lost their role of agencies of increasing 'civilisation', and instead have taken on the role of questioning and criticising. There are more or less extreme policy responses to this collapse of educational discipline and many people who agree with this tendency will regard this book as a god-send (or in their terms a God-send). The words of the youth of Sunderland, in their eyes, underline the results of liberalism. However, I have tried to stress the fact that moral values simply taught at an 'ideological level' do NOT openly affect people's actions. They do not become guides for action. I am not saying that this is the result of liberalism but it is the result of every education system that separates 'values' from the day-to-day material experience of the pupils. Thus this book may be used by the right as a pointer to the necessary change in direction lest we plunge over the abyss into moral anarchy. What is needed is a return to discipline in schools, and this must be enforced with as much force and with as many sanctions as necessary. Attendance must be ensured, with regular and systematic prosecutions for truancy. Once this has been enforced, then the school must set about the coherent and direct transfer of moral values to the pupils. The discipline within the school must be sufficient to make sure that these moral values are in fact transferred to the pupils. Like many right-wing solutions its very simplicity carries much conviction; but given the totality of my analysis it has a number of surprising results.

Most obviously such policies will not work simply by the pupils suddenly deciding to agree with them. To increase discipline in the schools, and to 'teach' correct moral values, will happen only if there is a massive increase in the number of teachers. It may be possible by application of a great deal of sanctions to terrify a class of forty into submission (though much of my research would contradict this) but it is *not* possible to 'teach' them moral values. To institute such discipline and to check the amount of success that the pupils have had in internalising these bourgeois values would take about twice as many teachers. It would also be necessary to institute such discipline in other areas of the lives of young people. It would be necessary to increase the number of police as well as of those social workers engaged in punitive activities with youth. To back up this regime of discipline it would be necessary to increase the number of children's homes for the failures of this localised discipline system. This would lead to an increase in public expenditure of massive proportions, which would contradict entirely the views of the groups and individuals who argue for an increase in school discipline.

And what would be gained? Let us suppose this was successful; that the pupils were terrified into a simplistic moral learning; that the pupils learnt that the world was simply ordered by discipline. This lesson that discipline was rigid would also have to be enforced in the world that the pupils experience outside school in their work. Here, only fear of greater power would be effective, and to enforce that would have massive repercussions for the whole of society. It is questionable whether the authoritarians could muster the force to carry this through.

The softer authoritarians recognise that force will not work for older pupils, and that these should be allowed to leave school as soon as they want to. Given the nature of the school that they have experienced between five and 14, it is likely that many of them would actually take this option willingly. This would mean that very few children would reach anything like the necessary educational standard for advanced technology; it would also mean that these people would hate education for the rest of their lives. This would be happening at a time when it is obvious that most school-leavers will be changing their jobs very often, requiring a great amount of retraining; such retraining needs a positive attitude to education on the part of the redundant workers. If a 27-year-old worker needs to be retrained, it is not helpful for him to see all education as rows of desks, and teachers teaching their own views as absolute truth.

The liberal soft centre

The new authoritarians have identified the existence of a group within education that they call the 'liberal establishment'. This group has managed to gain ideological control over the debate about educational method over the past 25 years. Being liberal they have *many* views on the matter of the increase in youthful disorder and educational method. Much of their argument centres around the denial that any major changes have occurred in the behaviour of youth. They claim that it is simply the *nature* of youthful disorder that has changed, both inside and outside school. Thus they point to a string of different post-war groupings of young men and women, showing the different fashions of this disorder; point to continuing violence at football matches over the history of football; the failure to prove any increase in juvenile crime. Inside schools they explain the change in behaviour as being a direct expression of different teaching methods; any new feeling of rebellion amongst schoolchildren is not actually harmful; rather it shows that they have the ability to formulate and express demands and activity. Such demands and activity rarely flow beyond the bounds of normal school behaviour and are therefore proof that the new teaching methods have allowed pupils to learn the right to express themselves.

Therefore this group combines a belief that there has been no major change in the extent of disorder with an attempt to say that it is all healthy in any case. The policy that flows from this is squarely based upon a consensus view of society, where the education system must become more open as a means of improving people's life chances. This education system needs no radical changes in it to be able to perform this task, rather it needs to become more open in its relationship with working-class children. The more radical of the 'liberal establishment' argue for a much greater stress on education relevant to the working classes as a method of reaching pupils, seeing this policy as a way of actually reaching pupils with an education that can move them in some useful way.

The ultra-left double bind

Since I carried out the field research reported earlier in this book, the positions occupied by various left groups have changed a great deal. Many more left parties have formulated policies on education which derive, in part at least, from the fact that some of their members are teachers who actually have to face the day-to-day struggle of classroom interaction. Consequently it is difficult to sum up simply the various left positions. Before trying to develop my own position I will, however, characterise two major elements in some of the more ultra-left positions.[1]

Much of the research work that was carried out on youth in the early 1970s was looking for a new group to identify as the vanguard of revolutionary change. For some of the left the working-class movement as a whole was either totally incorporated within the capitalist system or much too slow in their progress to revolution. Thus new groups were sought. One of the groups that the bourgeois press was constantly putting forward as threatening the very fabric of society was youth. Within the education system there was little real debate about the nature and form of education and all changes in the nature of the system were simply tinkering without changing the major power relationships of the school. Thus the ultra-left tend to see all 'new educational methods' as being so similar to the old ones as to make no political or social difference at all.

The only group which seemed to be consistently questioning the nature of education was the pupils themselves. People with radical positions of this kind will see in this research a number of signs that point to a resurgence of revolutionary feeling about education among youth itself; and perhaps see the working-class youth as capable of questioning, and maybe overthrowing, the conception of education inherent within capitalism, and replacing it with one that is much more capable of meeting the needs of working people. Indeed, personally I feel that there is much evidence for this in the words and actions of the Smash Street Kids in relation to schooling; it was they and not I who identified the major problem as being the state involvement in a *law* forcing them to go to school. It was they who saw both of my schools as being basically similar experiences even though they looked very different.

It is undoubtedly the case that the pupils were extremely stroppy about school and about their leisure activities; yet at no stage do they ever display anything but a *subordinate* consciousness in this struggle. By this I mean that they do not, and I believe by themselves cannot, formulate any conception of an alternative education system, of alternative uses of the school and spare time and, most obviously, of alternative forms of work for them when they leave school. Thus they are angry, but only within the bounds of the existing system of things. There are occasions when the new authoritarians can point to the Smash Street Kids as being on *their* side; and there are times when the ultra-left show them as being on their side.

One of the clearest phenomena to explain this is the dilemma that both groups have in coming to terms with punk rock. Both groups claim it as a sign that youth is on *their* side (though, to be fair to punks, they are very difficult to see as being in any way on the side of people like Rhodes Boyson). The right says that they are expressing some form of search for order in a world where they have been given too much freedom; that they represent an elemental cry for a return to that order. The left claims that they are the authentic voice of the working class laying the groundwork for the struggle for socialism by expressing the horrors of being young and living through a crisis of capitalism. Equally interestingly, there are groups on the left that characterise them in precisely opposite ways, seeing them as the new fascism, and there are also sections of the right that see punkers as final proof of the collapse of morality. In fact, like the Smash Street Kids when they say that they go to school because they have to, the punks are a true representation of life under a system which actually presents them with very little, except a struggle against odds. The consciousness that is formed within that struggle can take many forms, but rarely, if ever, can it pose clear alternatives to the totality of that experience. Thus the right is always jubilant when it finds pupils who say that they prefer Mr Jones because he is strict and 'you know where you are'. Such a consciousness represents simply the *only* alternative (within present experience) to the newer liberal teachers who exercise a liberal or democratic form of 'discipline'. The problem with seeing youth as the revolutionary vanguard, then, is their inability to pose alternatives which can be taken up by others in political terms. As a section of the working class, they represent their own interests; and they represent them in a fairly blinkered way. Thus their relationships with the local working-class community are far from harmonious.

The second focus for the ultra-left has been the relationship between the educational system and the capitalist system as a whole. Within a crude Marxism, the state and, therefore, the education system, represents an attempt to indoctrinate the working class ideologically. Again, much of my evidence from the nineteenth century backs up this formulation; yet the ultra-left argument goes further and is tighter than this. Since the society is capitalist, the state must be a capitalist state, therefore it must operate in the interests of capitalism. This means that the education system is *simply* a method of holding down the working class, which has obviously not overthrown capitalism (thereby proving the efficacy of the education system). Such a tight series of arguments means that any changes within the education system are politically unimportant. They ONLY represent changes in the tactics of the state and therefore of the ruling class in its *form* of ideological domination. The only way in which the education system will be changed is to make a total revolution, take over the state and change the nature of schools at that point. Thus they dismiss all the changes in technique as simply being attempts to stem a rising tide of youthful disorder, which itself represents a challenge to the capitalist system. This disorder they see as being caused by a crisis in the capitalist system itself, though they are usually unspecific about the mechanisms that relate that crisis to the experience of youth. This argument is extremely static and leaves very little if any room at all for the teachers themselves actually to do anything apart from simply oppressing their pupils (since that is their position as workers for the state). As a consequence, the educational politics that flow from this position simply seem to be waiting for the revolution.

Youth, class and revolutionary change

As I said previously, many of the groups have abandoned this position, at least in part because they had many teachers within their ranks who felt it was insufficient to define themselves simply as oppressors. This has combined with the growth that has occurred in Marxist analysis of the state to produce a distinctly different politics of education and one which I feel it is possible to tie into my research findings.

Firstly, it is very likely that there *has* in fact been a qualitative *and* quantitative change in the nature of youth behaviour over the past twenty years. It is impossible to be more explicit because youth studies are such a new activity within social sciences. But it would appear to be true that youth as whole is less accepting of everything it is offered. It is also probably true that working-class youth has begun to express this, at least as much if not more than its equivalent age group in the middle class, and that this expression *is* the 'youth revolt' that we constantly read about. The cause of this change can be found in the different demands that the totality of capitalist society (NOT just the schools) is making upon youth in the post-war period.

One of the characteristics that is increasingly being demanded of the whole labour force over this period is that it develop an ability to change jobs and skills. This has been necessitated by the increasing pace of change in the forms of work in factories and offices, the major skill that needs to be acquired now being the skill of changing your skill. How does this affect youth in particular?

In Marxist terms, any such change in the nature of production affects every aspect of society. Youth, being the labour force of the future, is affected most significantly by such changes. Thus the education system, the social services and many other aspects of the state will be affected by the fact that youth will have to undergo many changes within their lifetime, especially at work. (For example, it is no use the education system in Sunderland simply turning out people who are convinced that their future is intimately linked with either shipbuilding or mining for the rest of their lives, as these particular jobs will probably become out of date within twenty years. Similarly, it is ridiculous to bring up girls purely to be mothers, as their labour will on occasion be necessary in factories and in offices – that is, outside the home.)

Such changes may well be 'what capital needs' but it is not a simple matter to ensure that every aspect of society changes whenever capitalism requires it. Thus, to a large extent, the education system is required to teach flexibility, but presently the education system is constructed to teach inflexibility. Thus sections of education make contradictory demands upon youth as a whole; at one time pushing towards flexibility in the character; at another pushing people into pass/fail categories of an 'academic' kind and outdated social roles.

These contradictory messages give youth considerably more room for ideological manoeuvre than they experienced in the education system in the past. For the most part, though, this change in overall ideology has not been matched by any major changes in the *actual material room for manoeuvre* – that is, the youth labour market. Thus these purely ideological changes come into conflict with the much tighter objective reality of the labour market, a reality which is in no way constructed to meet the needs of youth itself.

The only place where there has been some real change in the possibility of action has been in the arena of youth as consumers. Whilst, from my research, the amount of money that youth actually has to dispose of is in fact not as great as is made out, they collectively represent a market to be exploited. As such they are the subject of advertising and the usual pressures on consumers that are the hallmark of a spending group in a capitalist society. (Noticed many adverts aimed at old people recently?) The consumer relationship is one where the individual is supposed to make tangible choices about what she or he wants. As such it is a relationship of individual 'rights' (as long as you have the money, that is). Such a relationship contradicts the lack of rights that the Smash Street Kids are also told is their position. Thus on the one hand they are treated as adult consumers, and on the other hand as children. Again this represents a contradiction in their experience as well as a feeling of wanting the consumer goods of a 'teenage lifestyle'.

Thirdly, these contradictions have not just been experienced passively. They have helped to create a culture that at least in part is the culture of the Smash Street Kids *themselves*. It is not simply 'their' music; but neither is it the record companies' music. Pop culture at least represents both of these. It does represent, and here my research findings are of crucial importance, an arena that is *theirs* more than it is their teacher's or their social worker's. It is a 'heartland' in which they can carry out aspects of their lives apart from the intrusions of powerful state employees. This provides them with a resource to draw on in which they can try and work out the sorts of contradictions that I have explained. Consequently it is ridiculous to say that youth culture causes unrest; but it is probably correct to say that it provides a cultural arena where that unrest can be worked through, even though it is not caused by it.

Therefore I have tried to show analytically why I believe that the youth of the United Kingdom has been placed in a series of contradictory positions as actual and potential labour and actual and potential consumers; and that this has provided them with ideological and occasionally material room to be different, yet for the most part not enough material room to express that difference, leading to clashes with morality and law. If so, what is to be done?

I do not see the contradictions that I have outlined as being at all reversible within capitalism. The new authoritarians would have to reverse the development of the forces of production within factories and offices to be able to commence stopping the movement for creating people capable of change. This is unlikely, though we must never rule out the possibilities of a fall into the barbaric fascism that would be necessary to carry this out. Such a change would appear to go against the sorts of trends that have led both Spain and Portugal out of that form of state power. Given that they are not reversible, what does this mean for us all? Do we then simply have to put up with increasing disorder in school, increasing vandalism, increasing problems?

In this work I think I have identified a large group of people in society (working-class youth) that sees itself as being pushed around in a way that is sometimes very humiliating and always quite confusing. I have identified that this group does not have either the consciousness or the political power to get out of this situation on its own. I have also identified political struggle on a much wider level as being the only overall solution to the problems that were forged by the political struggle of individuals such as Kay-Shuttleworth in the nineteenth century. What is important, then, is the nature of the political struggle that can be carried out to change the situation.

I am not saying that one should sit back and wait for a revolution, after which youth will be as free as birds and all will be sweetness and light. Rather I want to formulate a series of different actions by different sets of people that would assist youth in getting out of the situation. To start with those in the most difficult position: the teaching staff. The education system that they work in has been formed partly as an instrument to tie down working-class youth; the evidence of these Smash Street Kids is that it doesn't work too well in this function in the present period. This does not mean that this is all that education can or does do. Given the nature of contradictions within the present education system it IS possible to teach in a slightly more humane way, to reach pupils with a different view of the world than Kay-Shuttleworth would want. This teachers should try to do, yet it is wrong of them to *expect* their 'charges' to thank them for this change. As long as the overall relationship between the working class and the state (that is, that of subordination) remains the same then teachers will be placed in a position of too much power over their pupils (as indeed will university lecturers). Yet teachers should not simply accept that position as inevitable. They should be aware, as increasing numbers are, that any minor change in their difficult position will only come about if they join with political and social allies who are committed to change such a situation. This is not simply to say, work for the revolution and forget your education. Rather it is to say that any minor steps forward in their present position are going to need a great deal of political power to enforce or to hold. The isolation of the teaching profession and teachers from the labour movement on matters of 'professional competence' in educational terms will only lead to defeat; it is necessary for teachers to 'educate' *and* to listen to the rest of the working class about education. This is not impossible; indeed, much is being done in isolated cases to include parents, community organisations and political parties in discussions about the problems of education at the moment. These discussions go beyond simple questions of resources (vital though these are) to the whole nature of education in a capitalist society.

Secondly, the pupils themselves. They have some clear ideas about what is happening to them. Time and again the Smash Street Kids surprised me with the clarity of their understanding of the social relationships that created their problems. But by themselves it proved almost impossible for them to see a clear way out to any alternative. Yet crucially this does not mean that they are wrong; rather it means that the alternatives that they create must be incomplete and can only be subordinate. Yet it is very difficult to work with them about changes in the nature of, say, education when in fact they only want to get out of it. So it does become important for them to see some point in education itself; to see some point in the power that literacy and knowledge gives them. This they cannot be *forced* into; they have to be won to the importance of it, and it is here that some of the newer teaching ideas become important as a tactic to winning pupils to the importance of knowledge. How that tactic is used depends upon the overall political consciousness of the individuals and groups that are using it. That, mainly, depends upon the sorts of political struggles engaged in by teachers, as outlined above. In my own dealings with youth I see that tactic as winning them to a strategy which tries as much as possible to maximise the democratic demands that they make upon society and upon themselves, so that in the middle term they come to understand the social relationships that are shaping their lives, not to smash them tomorrow but rather to understand ways in which they might be changed and transformed. In my experience of the Smash Street Kids and others, this is not a difficult path to move along with them. Like many of the rest of us they experience being pushed around, and like most of us don't like it or understand how to change it on their own. They ARE interested in understanding it better and at least potentially in changing it for themselves and others.

What of the rest of us? Firstly, we must stop knocking both teachers and pupils; we must stop knocking social workers and clients; we must even stop knocking individual coppers and vandals and we must better understand the social forces that create the relationships rather than looking for scapegoats of the left or of the right. Secondly, in the terms that ended my research, we must realise the depth of the changes that are necessary to improve the situation in any real way. By this I mean a change in overall working-class consciousness and the situation that constructs that consciousness. But the left is guilty of seeing it as easy. It sees the revolution as a cathartic, explosive moment. After that it will be changed.

Rather, we must see the transformation of those social relationships as being a long-term process based upon the change in class consciousness. This means starting now. Both teachers and the Smash Street Kids are caught within the bounds of capitalism; it is necessary within the institutions of the capitalist state to raise issues and consciousness which will, in alliance with vast struggles throughout the whole of society, transform not only the schooling of the Smash Street Kids but also all social relationships of exploitation and oppression.

Such a solution may seem a long way away from truancy. If so, I am sorry, but blame the kids; they led me there. Such a solution may seem beyond the reader and more the responsibility of Great Men and Women, rather than being possible in the lives of ordinary folk. If so, I am sorry, but the burden that we all carry is to create history ourselves and to change the world so that history lessons are no longer about Great Men and Great Women, but more the story of you, me and the Smash Street Kids.

References

Chapter 1

1. B. Robson, *Urban Analysis: Sunderland* (Cambridge University Press, 1969) p. 75.
2. Newsom Report, *Half our Future* (London: H. M. S. O., 1963).
3. D. Hargreaves, *Social Relations in a Secondary Modern School* (London: Routledge and Kegan Paul, 1967) p. ix.
4. Ibid., p. 201.
5. Mao Tse-tung, *Oppose Book Worship* (Peking: Foreign House Press, 1930) p. 2.

Chapter 2

1. A. K. Cohen, *Delinquent Boys* (Chicago: Free Press, 1955).
2. D. Hargreaves, *Social Relations in a Secondary Modern School.*
3. J. Klein, *Samples from English Cultures* (London: Routledge and Kegan Paul) pp. 19–21.
4. J. Young, *The Drug Takers* (London: Paladin, 1971).
5. *The Times*, 2 September 1854.
6. See R. Johnson, 'Educational Policy and Social Control in Early Victorian England', *Past and Present*, 49; and P. R. D. Corrigan, 'State Formation and Moral Regulation in 19th Century Britain Sociological Investigations' (Durham Ph. D. thesis, 1977).
7. H. Tremenheere, *The State of the Population in the Mining Districts* (Report to the Board of Trade, 1844) p. 7.
8. Ibid., p. 13.
9. Ibid., p. 14.
10. Ibid., p. 13.
11. Ibid., p. 14.
12. Ibid., p. 7.
13. J. Kay-Shuttleworth, *Four Periods of Public Education* (London, 1862) pp. 231–2.

14. J. Kay-Shuttleworth, *Thoughts and Suggestions on Certain Social Problems* (London, 1868) p. 194.
15. I. Illich, *Deschooling Society* (Harmondsworth: Penguin, 1971).
16. F. Engels, 'The Condition of the English Working Class', in *Marx and Engels on Britain* (Moscow: Foreign Languages Publications, 1845) 2nd edn, p. 157.
17. Ibid., p. 157.
18. Minutes of the Council of Education, 1844, p. 430. Quoted in R. Johnson, 'Educational Policy and Social Control in Early Victorian England', *Past and Present*, 49.
19. Ibid., 1840.
20. Ibid., 1844, ii, p. 57.
21. Ibid., 1839–40.
22. R. Johnson, 'Educational Policy and Social Control in Early Victorian England'.
23. *Manchester Education and Society* (Manchester Education Aid Society, 1866).
24. W. Saunders, *Factory Inspector's Reports of 1835*, p. 156. Quoted in M. Thomas, *The Early Factory Legislation* (Leigh on Sea: Thames Publishing , 1948).
25. Ibid., p. 442.
26. See N. Young, 'Prometheans or Troglodytes? The English Working Class and the Dialectics of Incorporation', *Berkeley Journal of Sociology*, 12.
27. Robert Lowe quoted in A. Martin, *Life and Letters of the Rt. Hon. Robert Lowe* (London, 1893) vol. iii, p. 323.
28. R. Lowe, *Primary and Secondary Education* (London, 1867) pp. 9–10.
29. Ibid., p. 32.
30. Hansard, *Parliamentary Debates* (Commons) vol. 396, col. 211.
31. Newsom Report, *Half our Future* (London: H. M. S. O., 1963) para. 57.
32. Ibid., para. 199.
33. Ibid., para. 202.

Chapter 3

1. C. Lacey, *Hightown Grammar* (Manchester University Press, 1970); D. Hargreaves, *Social Relations in a Secondary Modern School* (London: Routledge and Kegan Paul, 1967).
2. C. Cox and A. Dyson (eds), *Black Papers on Education* (London: Davis-Poynter, 1971).
3. D. Hargreaves, *Social Relations in a Secondary Modern School*.
4. Ibid.
5. 'The Poetry of the Poor', *London Review* (1832) pp. 199–200.

6. B. F. Skinner, *Cumulative Record: A Selection of Papers* (Enfield: Appleton Century-Crofts, 1972) 3rd edn.

Chapter 4

1. E. J. Maizels, *Adolescent Needs and the Transition from School to Work* (London: Athlone Press, 1970).
2. R. Cloward and L. Ohlin, *Delinquency and Opportunity* (New York: Free Press, 1960) pp. 106–7.

Chapter 5

1. D. Downes, *The Delinquent Solution* (London: Routledge and Kegan Paul, 1966) p. 250.
2. J. B. Mays, *Growing Up in a City* (Liverpool University Press, 1954) p. 126.
3. D. Hargreaves, *Social Relations in a Secondary Modern School* (London: Routledge and Kegan Paul, 1967) p. 188.
4. I. Taylor, 'Soccer Consciousness', in S. Cohen (ed.), *Images of Deviance* (Harmondsworth: Penguin, 1971).

Chapter 6

1. See H. Parker, *View from the Boys* (Liverpool University Press, 1972).
2. J. Klein, *Samples from English Cultures* (London: Routledge and Kegan Paul, 1965).
3. J. B. Mays, *Growing Up in a City* (Liverpool University Press, 1954) p. 127.
4. A. K. Cohen, *Delinquent Boys* (Chicago: Free Press, 1955).
5. D. Downes, *The Delinquent Solution* (London: Routledge and Kegan Paul, 1966).
6. V. I. Lenin, 'What is to be Done?', in *Selected Works* (Moscow: Progress Publishers, 1970) vol. 2.
7. Mao Tse-tung, 'Essay on Practice', in *Four Essays on Philosophy* (Peking: Foreign Languages Press, 1968).
8. W. Whyte, *Street Corner Society* (Chicago University Press, 1943).
9. D. Downes, *The Delinquent Solution*, ch. 5.
10. D. Matza, *Delinquency and Drift* (New York: Free Press, 1964).
11. See J. Lambert, *Race and Police in Birmingham* (Oxford University Press, 1970); and J. Skolnick, *Justice without Trial* (Chichester: Wiley, 1966).
12. See D. Woodhill, *Whose Side are they on? Criminal Responsibility in the Juvenile Court* (Durham mimeographed paper, 1972).
13. E. Lemert, *Human Deviance: Social Problems and Social Control* (Englewood Cliffs: Prentice-Hall, 1967).

Chapter 7

1. For a further analysis see S. Frith and P. Corrigan, 'The Politics of Education', in M. Young and G. Whitty (eds), *Society, State and Schooling* (Lewes: Falmer Press, 1977).